PENGUIN BOOKS

# THE HIGH GIRDERS

John Prebble was born in Middlesex in 1915, but spent his boyhood in Saskatchewan, Canada. He entered journalism in 1934 and is now a novelist, a film-writer (*Zulu* amongst others), and the author of highly praised plays and drama-tized documentaries for television, including contributions to *Henry VIII* and *Elizabeth R*.

During the war he served for six years in the tanks with the Royal Artillery, from which experience he wrote his successful war novel *The Edge of Darkness* (1948). His other novels include *Where the Sea Breaks* (1944) and *The Buffalo Soldiers* (1959), which won an award in the United States for the best historical novel of the American West.

He has also written several books on the history of Scotland. These include *Culloden* (1961), a subject in which he became interested when he was a boy in a predomin-antly Scottish township in Canada. *Culloden* was subse-quently made into a successful television film. This was followed by its natural successors, *The Highland Clear-ances* (1963), *Glencoe* (1966), *The Darien Disaster* (1968), *The Lion in the North* (1971) and *Mutiny: The Highland Regiments in Revolt 1743–1804* (1975). (All of these books have been published in Penguins.) John Prebble is a Fellow of the Royal Society of Literature. He is married, with two sons and a daughter.

JOHN PREBBLE

# THE HIGH GIRDERS

## THE STORY OF THE TAY BRIDGE DISASTER

*'Appalling Catastrophe at Dundee'*

PENGUIN BOOKS

Penguin Books Ltd, Harmondsworth, Middlesex, England
Penguin Books, 625 Madison Avenue, New York, New York 10022, U.S.A.
Penguin Books Australia Ltd, Ringwood, Victoria, Australia
Penguin Books Canada Ltd, 2801 John Street, Markham, Ontario, Canada L3R 1B4
Penguin Books (N.Z.) Ltd, 182–190 Wairau Road, Auckland 10, New Zealand

—

First published in Great Britain by Martin Secker & Warburg Ltd 1956
Reissued by Martin Secker & Warburg Ltd, with foreword and new illustrations, 1975
Published in Penguin Books 1979

—

Made and printed in Great Britain by
Cox & Wyman Ltd, London, Reading and Fakenham
Set in Linotype Pilgrim

For

COLIN YOUNG

who
encouraged me
to write this

# CONTENTS

# ILLUSTRATIONS

# FOREWORD

THE enduring remembrance of a calamity like the Tay Bridge Disaster is not explained by the nature of the event alone, the damage done or the numbers dead. If that were so it would have been long since obscured by catastrophes of greater proportions now forgotten. It is remembered because its effect upon the compassion and complacency of the time was so great that an emotional shock-wave continues to pass through succeeding generations. It is almost a century since a great storm plucked the iron bridge from its stilts and sent it and a train into the Firth of Tay, yet the disaster is still a part of the nation's folk-lore, and although little or nothing may be known of the details a reference to it can produce a reaction of horror.

It is not the loss of seventy-five lives, an engine, five carriages and a brake-van, one thousand yards of iron girders. Nor yet the loss, within eighteen months of its completion, of the longest and greatest bridge in the world. Something more was destroyed in the darkness of those terrible seconds: the Victorians' smug pride in their industrial supremacy, their belief in their creative infallibility. Disasters on a colonial battlefield, at Kabul, Cawnpore or Isandhalwana, could be reversed by the punitive victories that always followed, but the self-conceit of the age never recovered from the fall of the Tay Bridge and the unnerving revelations of a Board of Trade Inquiry. It would be easy, then, for this age to see the disaster as a salutary lesson to the excessive hubris of the Victorians, were it not for the fact that the pride, greed, inefficiency and ignorance that contributed to the fall of the bridge are part of our way of life too.

*1974*                                        JOHN PREBBLE

# OVERTURE

*'Wait, wait, we'll see her soon!'*

SHORTLY before seven o'clock in the evening John Watt, a foreman surface worker in the employ of the North British Railway Company, went to share a can of tea with his friend Thomas Barclay.

It was not far from his cottage to the signal cabin, but the path led up the Fifeshire bank of the Tay and he found it hard to climb the wet earth against the pull of a south-westerly gale. This was a stronger wind than any Watt could remember. He felt it beating against his ears, taking the air from his mouth before he could suck it into his lungs. When he reached the shelter of the cabin he heard a restless thrumming along the latticed iron of the new bridge. Heavy clouds were fast-racing down the firth to the German Sea, and in the darkness below them the bridge was a thread of tiny lamps only, looped across the throat of the Tay. Now and then the wind tore a hole in the clouds, and a full moon shone on the black water and the black girders and the black nipple of Dundee Law.

Thomas Barclay's signal cabin was held in a fork where the single line left the bridge and turned eastward and westward. It was high in the wind and its northern windows faced across the Tay to the city of Dundee over a mile away.

The two men greeted each other and agreed that the weather was bad. The cabin was vibrating uneasily, and John Watt stood with his back to the stove and looked out of the window and said again that the weather was bad.

At eight minutes past seven o'clock the signal bell rang, and John Watt asked if this came from St Fort. Barclay said that it did, and that the 5.20 from Burntisland had left St Fort and would soon be at the bridge. He signalled the cabin on the northern bank, and within fifteen seconds his signal was acknowledged by one beat of the bell, and then two, and then a final beat. It was nine minutes past seven and Thomas Barclay recorded these times in his log book.

They felt the push of the gale against the cabin, and because it could be as bad as this in the lee of Wormit Bay where they were, they knew that it must be very bad out in the firth.

At twelve minutes past seven the train came along the westward turn. They saw it first as a flare against the darkness, a string of sparks drawn taut, and then smudges of uncertain light from six carriages. Barclay took a baton from its hole, and he opened the door of the cabin and went down the steps to the boarding.

The train passed him slowly, moving, as the regulations insisted, at no more than three miles an hour. Barclay walked alongside the engine for a few paces, and he saw the glare of the fire on the driver's white moleskin trousers, the black mark of a grin as the stoker leaned out to take the baton. Then Barclay halted and watched the carriages pass, and saw a face here and there looking down at him from the windows. Once it was a child's face.

He went back to the cabin, glad to be out of the wind. It was thirteen minutes past seven and he signalled to the northern box that the train was on the bridge. The acknowledgement came back promptly – one beat of the bell, and then two, and then a final beat. Thomas Barclay gave the clear signal to Wormit and he recorded the times in his log book.

The tension had passed, and he squatted down before the fire and raked out the dead coals.

From the north window of the cabin John Watt said 'There is something wrong with the train.' He said it calmly and without excitement.

John Watt had served the Company for twelve years against the three years and eight months of Barclay's service. But Barclay was a young man and jealous of his work, and proud that he had been signalman at the south cabin since the opening of the great bridge. He was quick to resent any suggestion that

Watt might know more about the bridge than he. He said 'Nothing has happened to the train, John.'

Standing by the window of the closed door Watt had watched the train as it gathered speed on the bridge. He saw the retiring sway of its three tail-lamps, and then, suddenly, he saw a spray of sparks from its wheels that grew and merged into a steady flame pulled eastward by the wind. He watched this curiously for three minutes until there were three distinct flashes and then one great flash. Then there was darkness. He could not see the tail lamps now.

He said 'The train's gone over, Thomas.'

Barclay got up from the fire and came to the window, holding his face against it and frowning.

'Her tail lamps have gone,' said Watt.

Barclay looked across the dark river and at last he said 'Of course her tail lamps have gone. She's gone down the incline to the north side. We'll seen her again soon.'

They waited, and Watt said 'I'm afraid something's happened to her, Thomas.'

'Wait,' said Barclay, 'Wait, we'll see her soon.'

He was impatient with the older man, and he took the scuttle and went down the steps for more coal. When he returned Watt was still watching the river and he said that he had not seen the train again. It was three minutes since he had said that the train had gone over, and Barclay now knew that something must be wrong.

He rang the bell to the north box and there was no acknowledgement. He tried both his speaking instruments and there was no reply.

Watt and Barclay looked at each other and did not know what to do, or how to say what they were thinking. Then, because they felt alone in this box of light and because they could not imagine what had happened outside in the darkness, they opened the door and ran down the steps. They stood on the boarding and the wind tore at them.

Instinctively they began to walk out along the bridge, and they halted after twenty yards for the wind had already forced them to their knees. They were afraid of being blown into the river, so they went back, and ran along the eastward turn and struggled down the bank to the shore of the Tay. They walked up and down, to the east and to the west side of the bridge, shielding their eyes from the wind and staring out across the river, and when they shouted at each other the wind snatched the sentences and broke them into meaningless words.

They saw nothing, until the moon came out, and then they saw.

The centre of the bridge was no longer there. The High Girders, thirteen spans through which the line had passed as through a tunnel, were gone, and the twelve iron columns that had supported them were gone too. One thousand and sixty yards of the great Tay Bridge were gone, and with them an engine, five carriages and a brake-van belonging to the North British Railway Company. Gone also were seventy-five men, women, and children.

This happened at approximately twenty minutes past seven on the evening of Sunday, 28 December 1879. It was the night of the Great Storm.

# ACT ONE

*'To raise their drooping shares'*

# I

## The River and a Man

NEAR the summit of Ben Lui, on its northern slope and three thousand feet above sea level, there is a great basin, glacier-cut and youthful by a geologist's calendar. Sheet-ice scooped it out a million years ago, and spread the debris along Strathmore, but the rocks of Ben Lui are more than a thousand million years in age, and are perhaps part of the first crust of this planet. Against this weary timelessness must be set the fifty-eight years lived by Sir Thomas Bouch who first bridged the mouth of the Tay.

For it is in a corrie at the upper end of the basin that the river springs from the earth. From October to June the Tay, which is not yet the Tay but sweet-sounding Allt an Rund, comes black and pure and cold from the snow, and a man may bridge it with his instep. One hundred and ten miles later it reaches Dundee, and there Sir Thomas' bridge was two miles long.

As with all rivers its gestation was slow, its beginning a minor grieving following a great terrestrial agony in which the land heaved and split. For a hundred and fifty million years Strathmore, the great valley, lay beneath the sea until it rose again. Rain fell on the harsh hills for days and weeks and years, and then there came the ice-sheets which, gripping great boulders beneath them, rasped out the Grampians. When the ice had gone the river ran down, building up lakes along the ice terraces and losing them when the land broke under the pressure. Cutting, fingering, pinching the land, laying up alluvial fertility in the valleys, swinging to all points of the compass, it reached at last the wide estuary where, sooner or later, a man would be forced by history, by economics, and by his own pride and ambition to build a bridge.

For the first eleven miles of its course the Tay runs rapidly, dropping two hundred and fifty feet with every mile, and moving more quickly than any river in Britain with the exception of the Spey. But with a tenth of its journey over it loses its impetuosity, runs in and out of the loch that gives it its name, and swings now sweetly and gently into Scottish tradition, drawing to it the water of a thousand lochans.

The river is like a child, losing its beauty and charm as it grows, but redeeming the loss in service to those who love it. The Tay that sings through ice-hewn glens, frothing brown from violet rocks to silvered grass, skirting the history that was cut by broadswords at Killiecrankie, Birnam and Dunkeld, meets the green tidal flood at Perth, and widens there to become a great firth, twenty-four nautical miles in length. It loses is vigour as it slides to the sea over a gravel bed, but there it becomes a harbour, and harbours are for men. The river made Dundee the industrial capital of the north. It made the men of Dundee proud and stiff-necked in their independence, until the coming of the railways humbled them, and they were forced to throw a bridge across the Tay or see that independence change to isolation. The firth that had blocked the legions of Agricola and the armoured cavalry of the Normans, became an obstacle to the export of jute, jam and journalists.

A century and a half ago the Tay gave the eastern Highlands their prosperity. Its water is pure and soft, free from dissolved salts, particularly lime, made in the Lower Palaeozoic Age for the bleaching and dyeing industries. There are three or four grains of dissolved salts only to a gallon of Tay water, and this is fine if you are a bleacher or dyer.

On its upper reaches the Tay is for the salmon and the wag-tails, the whin-chat, red-breast, reed-warbler and corbie. For the fox, red deer and long-tailed field mouse. Its mouth is for the seal, sand-piper and black-backed gull. Pearl-mussels once grew in the gravel of the estuary, offering stones that were white or deep brown, and sometimes beautifully iridescent. The kings of Scotland added such stones to their daughters' dowries when they married the girls to Scandinavian princes. The mussel-dred-gers knew the bed of the Tay as a farmer knows his fields, and this knowledge was of value to them, even when the pearl-mussels began to disappear. They knew just where the swing of the river or the swirl of the tide would take a drowned man. Of the seventy-five men, women and children who went down into the Tay with the bridge and the 5.20 from Burntisland, many were later recovered by the hooks of the mussel-men. For this service the North British Railway Company offered £5 a body.

In the thousands of years that men lived along the lower valley of the Tay, once they had crawled north behind the retreating ice, they knew the bitter anger of the weather in the firth. The winds that blew from the west and the south-west were funnelled between narrow hills that urged the gales on to speeds of seventy and eighty and ninety miles an hour. The Tay joined in this great tumult, leaping and heaving like an ocean. Once men had built the city of Dundee these western gales ripped tiles and chimney-cairns from the roofs, picked stones from hillside walls, broke windows, sank ferry-boats. In the great gale of 1859 the lanterns of the navigation lights at Tayport vibrated so terribly that the nails and the bolts and the light-house keeper's reason were all unseated.

So it is odd that Sir Thomas Bouch paid little attention to wind pressure when he designed his bridge.

Of him we know less than we know of the river. There is scarcely a feature of the Tay that was not patiently recorded in the eighteenth and nineteenth centuries by those clerks in holy orders who relieved the boredom of office by becoming amateur topographists, geologists, archaeologists.

For example: speeding past Perth at 3.09 miles an hour the Tay discharges a mean of 207,000 cubic feet of water a minute. Its temperature in December will be 35.9°F, in August it will be 55.5°F. The tide can raise its level over 19 feet, and the current of flood-tide at Dundee is so strong that the level of the river on the north bank is two to three inches higher than on the south bank. The bed of the firth, geologically speaking, is Old Red Sandstone, Upper Palaeozoic Era, with an age of fifty million years or so, and betraying it here and there by the fragile imprint of a prehistoric sea-lily, a hundred feet below the water and the gravel. The stone floor is covered by a deep blanket of mud and sand and stones, much deeper than Thomas Bouch believed when his first borings were made. What Mr Wylie, who performed this service, told him was bedrock was in fact an obstinate belt of gravel.

Against such a clear knowledge of the river that vanquished him the reflection which Thomas Bouch throws on history is almost in silhouette only. There should be no particular regret at this, for in view of the final tragedy of his life it would be uncharitable to stare at him naked. Half-light and half-knowledge are compassionate at our distance. Yet, it is as if he had offended the pride of nineteenth-century British engineering by proving that it was not infallible, and that because of this there has been a deliberate conspiracy to erase his memory.

If this were so, and it is not, it would be unjust. British engineers of the last century not only seemed capable of appalling mistakes, but were remarkably diffident about them. When a bridge built by Brunel collapsed he is said to have remarked 'I am very glad, I was just going to build a dozen like it.' When a sea-wall, that had cost £10,000, was washed away by a storm at Sunderland docks, the engineer said 'Very good, very good indeed! It will help to consolidate the works.' And a British Engineer in India, who narrowly escaped accompanying his 25-span bridge when the waters of the Nerbudda carried it away, observed that the disaster was 'a grand illustration of the destructive power of the elements.'

If Thomas Bouch did not take his failure as lightly as this it was because he was a lonely, single-purposed man with very little in his life but the building of bridges. He began with little viaducts that are still as graceful as they are serviceable, and he ended with a slender iron ribbon that was the longest bridge in the world. Most seemingly impossible schemes appear ridiculously possible once executed. The sad oddity of Thomas Bouch's bridge was that it looked impossible even when built.

But Bouch believed he had been born for something like this bridge. Ambitious men, whose work is creative, believe that they have been placed in the world to do something that had never been done before, and for twenty years Bouch had no doubt that his bridge across the Tay was inevitable, as, perhaps, the knighthood that conventionally rewarded him was inevitable too. The bridge fell down. If he could not give his knighthood back to Queen Victoria he could at least return his life to his Maker, which is more or less what he did.

Architects and engineers are among the most fortunate of men, since they build their own monuments with public consent, public approval, and often public money. Most of these monuments endure so long as men have need for them or respect for them. Thomas Bouch's self-constructed monument consists of a row of water-worn stumps jutting green at low tide along the east side of the present Tay Bridge. At that, few other men can have so dramatic a memorial.

His origin was little different from others of his generation who found position and power in the new age of iron and steam. His parentage was conventionally humble, with squirearchy in its lineage. Bouch was, and is, a Cumberland name, and it once bore arms – *or, on a cross sable five escallop shells apart.* The shells proved that somewhere in the past there had been a Bouch who went on a pilgrimage and wished everybody to know it.

Thomas Bouch's father was a retired sea-captain whose third son, the bridge-builder, was born in the village of Thursby, Cumberland, in 1822. He seems to have been an idle lad with talents that remained unawakened until one day the village schoolmaster began to explain how men had contrived to make water run uphill. Thomas Bouch at once took to reading books on Mechanics, or so his obituaries claimed.

Certainly, at the age of seventeen, he was apprenticed to a Carlisle engineer who was building the Lancaster and Carlisle railway. It was not entirely fortuitous that Bouch's introduction to engineering should be concerned with railways. There was hardly an engineer in the country who was not, in one form or another, flushed by the great fever. The growth of aviation in this century has not been more exciting or rapid than the expansion of the railways between 1830 and 1850. In those twenty years the social and economic body of Britain was transformed by the growth of a new nerve system. For the first time since the Romans, men demanded that the shortest distance between two points be a straight line, an iron line that went through hills and over rivers, that threw up embankments and straddled streets with arching brick-work. In one decade the civil engineer became the tribal shaman of a new religion that spoke its creed in terms of stress and strain. Any novitiate in an engineering office could promise himself riches and power before he was thirty.

A month before his twenty-seventh birthday Thomas Bouch, such a novitiate, became the manager and engineer of the Edinburgh and Northern Railway. Within a week he had seen the wide estuaries of the Tay and the Forth and declared his conviction that they could and should be bridged. It was, of course, laughable, so the stockholders laughed.

But if they would not let him build his bridges they allowed him to play with the idea of train ferries across the firths. It was not entirely his own idea, as nothing he ever did was entirely his own idea. He admitted that he had heard two other engineers discussing the possibility. One of these was Thomas Grainger, onetime engineer to the Edinburgh, Perth and Dundee Railway, who had in fact drawn designs for a floating caisson that would ferry wagons across the Tay between Broughty and Port-on-Craig.

With the imaginative recklessness that was always hidden behind an emotionless face, Bouch designed and executed a floating railway whereby goods wagons could run on to steam ferries from a flying bridge. Its details are unimportant here; what is important is that the success of his train-ferries established him as a most important man in the railway industry. He began to grow a beard, the flowing panache of the Victorian arrivé. The stockholders in his company, realizing that they might now compete with more important rivals, could not do enough for the young man (short of letting him build those bridges). They made so much of him, in fact, that he found it more profitable still to retire from their service and set himself up in his own engineering office.

Not everyone was full of admiration for the Cumberland lad. It was suggested that the Tay ferries were only an imitation of Robert Stephenson's steam ferry over the Nile. It was suggested still further that Thomas Bouch's talent owed more to rule of thumb than scientific knowledge. Such criticisms, which come inevitably to a rising man, acted on Bouch's nature as the gentlest touch does on a sea-anemone. It contracted. He developed a morbid dislike of publicity, and a profound distrust for the Press. He sensed irony, or at least hypocrisy, behind the compliments paid him, and when asked to reply at a dinner in his honour he stood uncertainly to his feet, fastened his distant-searching eyes on the ceiling, murmured 'Gentlemen, I thank you,' and sat down again.

Yet he was honest with himself, and if his critics had not been so anxious to say it at first he would have freely admitted his indebtedness to others. To Robert Stephenson, who altered Bouch's design for the Hownes Gill viaduct, thus increasing its stability. To Robert Bow, who deserves much credit for the Beelah Viaduct that was erected under Bouch's name.

But he was a busy man, and nothing was too small for him to design, and nothing too large, whether it was a culvert crossing for the five-mile Leslie Railway, or the Redheugh Bridge with its four spans, two of 260 feet and two of 240 feet.

Behind all his busy work with bricks and iron, his mind was still thinking of a bridge across the Tay, and thinking further of another across the Forth that could have spans 1,600 feet in length, strung a hundred feet above the river. When he designed the Tees bridge, with its stone piers and lattice girders, he was already experimenting, for when it was completed it closely resembled his later designs for the south sections of the Tay Bridge. With some justice he claimed the credit for the use of malleable iron lattice girders. They made, he said, a structure 'offering less resistance to the wind'. That was an odd phrase, as if his ear had caught some half-understood warning of the terrible winds that could blow down the Tay in the winter months.

A member of the Institution of Civil Engineers, his knowledge of mathematics seems to have been little better than that now needed to drag a child through the Higher Schools Certificate. He knew this, although he would permit no one to say that they knew it too. But he knew, and for all his pride he was not above taking advice from someone else. This someone was, inevitably, Robert Stephenson, who had become the Oracle of Engineering as a result of his tubular bridge over the Menai Strait.

'As a rule,' said Bouch many years later, when the public had his dying body in the witness box at Westminster Hall, and was relentlessly pricking a spirit already bruised by the fall of his wonderful bridge, 'I have almost always taken the depth of a girder an eighth of the span, and I was very much led into doing that from a conversation with Mr Robert Stephenson.'

'It facilitated the calculations,' he said.

It came as a surprise to the public to discover that these calculations were not the work of Sir Thomas Bouch but of an engineer in his employ called Allan Stewart. Mr Stewart had taken his degree at Cambridge.

It would be uncharitable to see Bouch as a man who designed a bridge that cost over £300,000 and ninety-five lives, twenty in the building of it and seventy-five in its fall. If his profession today speaks of him as a man whose ability was largely a skill in 'putting a bit on here and taking a bit off there,' he is entitled to be remembered as the man who made Fifeshire a railway highway, who designed nearly three hundred miles of railway in Scotland and the north of England, who built more bridges than any other man in his age. And if it be remarked that a bridge he built over the Esk at Montrose also fell down, then this was a small affair, a routine commission and not the realization of a dream. In any case, there was no train crossing the Esk at the time.

But seventy-six years have buried the man under statistics of bridges and brickwork, of pressure per square foot and weight per square yard. He is a tragic shadow behind barometrical measurements and anemometer readings. Whatever we could learn about his final agony will always be obscured by the number of elastic-sided boots that the mussel-dredgers hooked from the Tay after the disaster.

The oblivion that now hides him should also protect him, but does not. The journal of his profession, sixty years after his death, could still show that sense of betrayal all engineers felt at the fall of the Tay Bridge. He was, the words read, 'a recklessly ambitious engineer, possessing an incomplete knowledge of the forces with which he had to deal.'

The human being he was, the staunch Liberal and devout Episcopalian, exists in a few lukewarm pictures only. Of a medium-built, upright man baring his head in prayer on the day his bridge is begun. Standing in the wind at Wormit, holding his hat with one hand, his son's shoulder with the other. His eyes search the little crowd closely, as if he suspects that the hated Press had disguised itself as a workman and is present against his wishes.

The picture of an older man, with the fat of success and middle-age beneath his broadcloth now, riding to Windsor in the company of Henry Bessemer to receive his knighthood, and saying nothing of interest on the journey out and nothing of interest on the journey back.

The picture of a man so obviously dying that the public gallery sighs sharply as he enters to give evidence before an official inquiry into the disaster. It is only an inquiry, but because of those seventy-five dead he is as much on trial as Warren Hastings and Charles I who have stood in this hall before him. He faces examination with an iron, ungiving patience that breaks once only into the defensive cry 'I am explaining ... !'

When he died the nation wrote his obituary briefly, with an air of being glad to get something from its conscience. His widow lived quietly on the income from his capital and took to drink for reasons of her own. She then married a sea-captain.

# II

*'This proposed rainbow bridge'*

THERE was an old man who lived along the Carse of Gowrie, below the southward-falling braes of the Sidlaws. He had been born in the eighteenth century and he was gifted with an irascible foresight on all matters concerning his own affairs and those of others. This gift, which may have been the natal present of a Highland mother, was extraordinarily active. In Dundee he was known as 'The Seer of Gourdie', and he was laughed at whenever he communicated his prescience to the Press. The laughter merely moved him to greater clairvoyance.

He grew fine apples in his orchards at Gourdiehill, and he wrote brassy trumpet warnings to all and any who believed it possible to throw a bridge across the Firth of Tay.

The letters are all that is left of him now, so one may paint a picture of him that fits them, and possibly there is nobody to question its accuracy. Maybe he was a tall man and thin, yes, he must have been a tall man and thin, with a complexion as brown and wrinkled as one of his fallen apples, and a mane of white hair framing his querulous nose and mocking eyes. He was old, and must have worn a Highland plaid, that would have been of his mother's tartan, as he sat in his study to write his angry letters. Throughout the quarrels and arguments that preceded the building of the bridge he played a Greek chorus of irony and ridicule and bucolic amusement. His scorn punctuated the irritable squabble between the North British Railway and the Caledonian Railway. And the most disturbing thing about his major prophecy is that it came true.

In 1849 young Thomas Bouch came up to Scotland to be the traffic manager and engineer to the Edinburgh and Northern Railway, which subsequently became the Edinburgh, Perth and

Dundee, and was ultimately absorbed by the North British. The broad estuaries of the Tay and the Forth, water barriers across the approach to the north-east by road or rail, acted on Bouch's imagination with promptness. If pressed he could no doubt have used arguments that stressed the economic value of breaking down these barriers, in fact he did use such arguments when he first suggested to the Scottish North Eastern Railway that it build a bridge across the Tay at Dundee. But the simple reason for his enthusiasm was that he was a dreamer, and the most determined type of dreamer who must build what he dreams. Perhaps in the darkness at night he already believed it built, and could have put out his hand from the sheets and touched its cold iron and masonry. All creative work has its greatest reality while it is still in a man's mind, before he begins to execute it.

By 1854 the North British, in its ambition to embrace all Scotland within its steel arms, had taken over the Edinburgh, Perth and Dundee, and Bouch took his plan to his new directors. He was told that it was 'the most insane idea that could ever be propounded.' It was no less insane now than it had been a decade or so before when another nameless engineer had made the same suggestion. In this, as in so many things, Bouch had not produced an original idea. This director and that smiled tolerantly as Bouch left their offices, and they probably thought that they had heard the last of the matter.

When word of the idea reached Gourdiehill, Patrick Matthew reached for his pen. An earthquake, he thought, would surely bring down the bridge. He had frequently felt earth tremors while walking in his orchards. In his mind he could see the river-bed heaving angrily to rid itself of this impertinent burden. Or, he believed . . .

'. . . some vessel, drifting at anchor in a gale, or from the carelessness of a drunken crew, will run foul of and carry away the bridge.'

The citizens of Perth had no such visions of disaster. They were afraid that the bridge would be a success. The Tay was their highway to the world. For centuries ships of all countries had anchored off Perth, and if this custom was now dying quickly it only increased Perth's desire to preserve it. To have its sea-traffic blocked by a bridge was, in the opinion of Perth, an unsubtle attempt at murder that could be expected of the money-grubbers of Dundee.

The Caledonian Railway, the Scottish North Eastern and the Scottish Central who, between them, drained all traffic from the north-east Highlands to the south, were resolutely opposed to anything that would bring the North British across the Tay into their country.

In fact, all arguments for and against the building of the bridge in the twenty years that preceded its erection, can be viewed only in the perspective of the long struggle between the Caledonian and the North British. They fought for the domination of Scotland. It was a ruthless, worthless and sometimes comic war.

Both companies had been born in the mid-forties, distant spawn from the fertile genius of that rogue speculator George Hudson, who, whatever else might be said of him, at least had a vision of a great central railway system instead of a cloud of gadflies trying to run their railways like stage-coach lines.

When the two companies settled down to fight, the Caledonian was swinging up from the Border to Glasgow. The North British curved up the east of the Lowlands to Edinburgh. They held Scotland between finger and thumb, pinching out the smaller lines, and the only fault in this analogy is that the thumb and finger were not members of the one hand.

When the North British acquired the Edinburgh, Perth and Dundee it was already reaching for the north-eastern Highlands. And there it was blocked, for the Caledonian, in one of the most brutal struggles in railway history, had swallowed many of the little lines and now sat smugly across the path of the North British.

If, in those days, railways fought like children they at least had a child's honesty of definition. They did not disguise their struggle with the fine words by which industry now cloaks its amoral greeds. A war was a war, and was described as such. Thus, in 1854, the directors of the Caledonian Railway addressed

a letter to their shareholders, and instructed that it be published
in the press.

'With the utmost reluctance we have been driven to begin
active hostilities against your late ally, the Edinburgh and Glasgow Railway. All attempts on our part to bring about an agreement for and equitable division of traffic common to the two
lines are resolutely opposed ... [The Edinburgh and Glasgow]
has commenced a series of aggressions. We shall discontinue
hostilities when our opponents treat us with fairness.'

The struggle went on for years, and was ended only when
the North British took over the Edinburgh and Glasgow and
fought its battle for it. In any case the little line could not have
hoped for victory. It appears to have been a pious, God-fearing
railway, if such a thing is possible. It ran no trains on Sundays
and closed all its stations, thus loyally contributing to that air of
melancholy inaction that hangs over Scotland on the seventh
day. Whatever approval this may have won it was adroitly
overturned by the Caledonian, which accused it of deliberately
preventing people from visiting the country on their one day of
leisure, of forcing them to stay indoors, and 'thus compelling a
large consumption of whisky on the Sabbath'.

Through the 'fifties the North British watched the growth of
the Caledonian with much uneasiness. Once the Caledonian's
influence reached the cities of Perth, Dundee and Aberdeen, and
it began to live off the land north of them, the North British
knew that its chance of reaching across the Tay and sharing the
plunder was hopeless. The holders of Ordinary stock in the
company were impatient men, and this is understandable in
view of the fact that they often went without a dividend. They
were Englishmen for the most part, and were beginning to
wonder who it was that had advised them to invest in railways.
They were suspicious of a board composed of Scotsmen, since
this was before the days when men accepted, without argument, the proposition that a Scotsman was a better business
man than an Englishman. North British shareholders regarded
their directors as improvident money-wasters.

Consequently, when Thomas Bouch first deposited his plans

for a bridge across the Tay, the directors of the North British
may have thought it excellent, but were halted by the realization that they had not got the £200,000 to pay for it.

The argument for the bridge was indisputable. To travel from
Edinburgh to Dundee was an experience which, once at-
tempted, was not repeated if the passenger could think of an
alternative. Between him and his destination lay two wide
estuaries to be crossed by ferry, and in winter this part of the
journey needed a strong stomach and a lethargic imagination.

With that malignant sadism of which only the compilers of
railway time-tables seem capable, the best train of the day left
Waverley station, Edinburgh, at 6.25 a.m. The whole journey
was no more than forty-six miles, but it took three hours and
twelve minutes to complete it, or more if there were storms on
the Tay or the Forth.

If the travellers had not eaten before leaving home they stood
in shivering groups in the buffet room at Waverley, where certain standards had already been established, for the coffee, according to William Morris, was 'ineffably bad'. The train, ill-
heated and trailing two fish trucks, then took them to Granton
on the Forth where they boarded a ferry. These were graceful
boats, low in the hull, with beating paddles on either side, raking
masts, and high, slender smoke-stacks. From the shore they appeared to be resting lightly on the water like dragon-flies, but
aboard them, in a half-gale, the passengers leant sickly against
the bulkheads with their ears full of the remorseless splash of
the paddles, and their nostrils full of the stench of fish.

At Burntisland a train took them the thirty-six miles northward to Tayport on the south shore of the Tay estuary. There
another boat took them across to Broughty Ferry, where a third
train took them into Dundee, and very happy they all were to
be done with the whole wretched business.

Thus it did not require a dreamer like Thomas Bouch to see
that a fast express, running uninterrupted from Edinburgh to
Dundee, crossing the Forth and the Tay by bridge, was infinitely
preferable to the agony of the ferry system.

But the building of bridges costs money, and whenever the

directors of the North British thought about money they thought of their English shareholders and the problem of an Ordinary dividend. Many of these shareholders also held Caledonian stock, and were not above pointing out at the half-yearly meetings that whereas they received some return from their Caledonian holdings they could not always say the same for their North British.

Now and then a far-sighted shareholder, who perhaps realized that the only chance of enjoying his North British stock would come from such an ambitious scheme as the bridges, wrote to the Press and said so. Then the Seer of Gourdie turned from the contemplation of his apple trees. A bridge? Iron and brick to be set up against God's will?

'The tremendous impetus of the icy blast must wrench off the girders as if they were a spider's web, or hurl the whole erection before it.'

By an odd coincidence this sort of thing seemed to occur in winter, when the wind was doing its best to demonstrate what Patrick Matthew meant.

The Caledonian's opposition to the bridge was based on a firm belief in its possibility. Once built, such a bridge would make the North British master of eastern Scotland. The Caledonian's strategy was therefore designed to weaken the North British in a war of attrition, to force it year by year to postpone a decision.

The war increased in intensity during the sixties. The Caledonian absorbed the Scottish North Eastern, thus placing itself firmly across the Tay. It was apparent that there was going to be a vicious and merciless struggle with the North British, so apparent that, under Act, a special arbitrator was appointed to settle their differences.

Not that he did, but Cornelius Willes Eborall had a very busy five years.

It was a simple, straightforward war, its tactics clear. If one company built a line between points A and B, then the other company built one also. Passenger and goods rates were lowered, and lowered again, the condition of rolling stock became

deplorable. Company servants brawled in public on the station
platforms, and North British shareholders who also held shares
in the Caledonian now complained bitterly that 'our left hand is
fighting our right'.

Mr Eborall's decisions were made with such fine impartiality
that he was heartily detested by both sides.

The Caledonian deprived the North British of much of its
passenger traffic from the north of Scotland by refusing to allow
North British booking-clerks the use of a room in Caledonian
stations. The North British went to Mr Eborall, who said that he
could see no reason why the North British should not have such
facilities at Dundee, and that this must be so.

Whereupon the Caledonian sent a task-force of clerks to
invade Waverley Station and secure for it similar privileges. Mr
Eborall said that they had a right to be there and must stay.
Chagrined, the North British then demanded right of way for
its goods traffic over Caledonian lines between Greenhill Junction and Perth, and this, too, Mr Eborall granted.

Faced with a persistent uneasiness about each other's intentions the two companies adopted a system of espionage that had
only one weakness. The spy was also the counter-spy.

He was a clerk called Dykeson who had been placed in the
Caledonian's offices by the North British, with instructions to
keep it well-informed. Finding this profitable he offered his services to the Caledonian, saying that he was able to supply it
with information about the North British. After he had almost
produced a stalemate in the war he over-reached himself, was
discovered, and discharged.

For a while, in 1866, there was a dispirited effort to establish a
truce. Bewildered shareholders with money in both companies,
alarmed by the Caledonian's determination to 'blister the backs'
of its enemy, petitioned their directors to agree to a truce. Each
company appointed its delegates, sober, deliberate gentlemen in
black broadcloth and Tennysonian beards, who met in a flurry
of paper and promises. They drew up a formidable agreement,
allocating spheres of influence, areas of control, as if it were the
Treaty of Utrecht they were signing. Like all such agreements,

in politics or industry, it read handsomely. But it scarcely altered the situation, for within a year hostilities had broken out again.

The North British was sick in the limbs. At its half-yearly meetings shareholders shouted angrily from the floor, the meaning of their words lost in apoplectic indignation, and the chairman's gavel beat uselessly against the noise they made. Once, in lieu of a dividend it would appear, the Ordinary shareholders received a tastefully-printed map of the Company's network, a work of some delicacy admired by the directors and by no one else.

In one year the Caledonian was able to increase its profits by £23,461, against a loss of £3,009 by North British.

Thomas Bouch, in his forties now, and appearing older behind his greying beard, continued his practice of calling on North British directors to talk about his bridge. He was listened to with more politeness, for the Company was now like a sick man who gets some comfort from thinking of his remedy, although he may be in no position to pay for it.

Thomas Bouch came carrying long rolls of cartridge paper tied with pink tape, figures of stress and strain, figures of rivets, and bricks and cement and river-borings. But he did not know where to find the money.

Yet the answer was simple. If the jute and flax merchants of Dundee, the farmers of Forfar were to be connected with the Fife shore, and to be set within reach of Edinburgh, why should they not pay?

In Dundee there was a solicitor called Thomas Thornton, an intelligent man who had none of Bouch's extravagant dreams but who was jealous of his city's prosperity and aware of the great industrial earthquake that was roughly changing the contours of Britain. He called a meeting in his office.

It was a Friday, and it was October, and the Tay was a still sheet of yellow metal indistinguishable from the fog that hung down Dundee Law like a shawl. In the lawyer's office was Provost Parker and a sprinkling of jute and flax manufacturers, bleachers and dyers, who did not care one way or the other about the irritating squabble between the two railway companies, except in so far as it affected their businesses. They listened to Thomas Bouch, and perhaps yawned through his talk of malleable iron girders, and the relationship between the height of a span and its length. What they wanted to know was *could* such a bridge be built, and if it could what would it cost them and what return could they expect? None of these questions seems to have been answered satisfactorily.

That was in 1863, and although it was a meeting of some significance, in that it was the first time that the proposed bridge had moved from Thomas Bouch's imagination to a committee table, it proved nothing and proposed nothing.

A year passed to another October and to a public meeting in the Council Chamber at Dundee, presided over by Baillie Yeaman, but inspired and planned once more by Thomas Thornton. It was a larger meeting; now in addition to the big merchants there were small shopkeepers like Mr Phin, the grocer of Perth Road, who thought he owed his presence to his civic pride.

Bouch stood up before them all, flanked by a water carafe and his roll of designs, and tried to answer such questions as: *will it fall down as Mr Matthew says?* and *How much will it cost?*

'It is a very ordinary undertaking,' said Bouch, not, perhaps, because he believed this but perhaps because constant opposition to his dream had forced him to understate its magnitude when speaking of it, 'and we have several far more stupendous and greater bridges already constructed.' He did not say where, and it is strange that no one thought of asking him.

'I have estimated the cost at £180,000,' he said, 'I will stake my professional reputation that the cost will not exceed this amount.' This was a very high stake, and placing it was one of those wild misjudgements of which Bouch was capable.

There was generous applause. There was even more applause when James Cox, who was one of Dundee's richest citizens, and its largest employer of labour, was suddenly warmed by Bouch's enthusiasm and declared his support for the scheme, declaring it in a most convincing manner. He said that he was prepared to put his money into it. This was something that the men of Dundee could understand.

'RESOLVED ...' agreed the Town Councillors and the bankers and the jute merchants and the flaxspinners and the grocer from Perth Road '... that it would be for the public advantage, and tend greatly to the traffic of the North of Scotland and specially the town and trade of Dundee, were the present inconvenient and expensive route to the south improved by the construction of a bridge across the River Tay, and were suitable provision made for a general passenger station at Dundee; and that a Committee be appointed to consider and promote the scheme.'

A week later the public was offered the prospects of the Tay Bridge and Dundee Union Railway Undertaking. It had a proposed capital of £350,000 in 14,000 shares of £25 each.

A snort of contempt came down by the next mail from Gourdiehill. '*This proposed rainbow bridge* ...!' said Patrick Matthew.

He had chosen the wrong word. A rainbow catches the imagination, it does not destroy it.

On the fifteenth day of November 1864, Parliamentary notice was given of a Bill to provide for the incorporation of the company. The Bill also provided for the construction of the bridge and its connecting lines, and, *inter alia*, it gave power to the North British Railway Company to subscribe to the capital. The North British appears to have appreciated this gesture without making any promises.

At once the Caledonian awoke to the danger. Flushed with its little victories over the North British, it had believed this plan for a bridge would never get beyond Thomas Bouch's drawing table. Now, suddenly, it was blossoming quickly. The directors of the Caledonian sat down to assess the opposition to the scheme.

It was formidable. The Dundee Harbour Board, many of the Trustees of which were Town Councillors, not unnaturally resented a future in which goods might be brought in and out of the city by rail instead of by sea. The Harbour dues were high, and the Board was prosperous, and this was a state of affairs they wished to keep unchanged.

The Scottish Central and the Scottish North Eastern Railways, who controlled the north of the Tay, with a future already darkened by the spreading wings of the Caledonian, had no wish to see the claret and cream carriages of the North British coming across the river also.

Finally there was the City of Perth, ancient capital of Scotland, and, like all those with threadbare dignity, quick to take offence. The rivalry between Perth and Dundee was old, and if it was no longer expressed by the ring of broadsword on targe, or the dust-trail of pikemen, it was still deep-rooted and bitter. The tide turned at Perth, but yet the city looked upon itself as a sea-port. The bridge would be a dam that destroyed it.

The Caledonian lobbied enthusiastically among such opposition. On the Dundee Council it found many head-shakers and lip-curlers, many men with heavy investments in the Caledonian itself. Suitably stimulated they began to voice their opposition to the scheme with some heat. They said, cannily, that they liked fine the idea of a bridge, but did not believe it was possible to built one two miles long. Or, if it were possible, why should it be the monopoly of one railway only, why should not others have interest? There were afraid that the desire to build such a bridge sprang more from pride than common sense.

In this last belief they were supported by the Seer of Gourdie. 'The grandeur and difficulty more than the utility and wisdom of the enterprise fascinates the movers of the scheme.'

A shrill voice came from the back of the protests. The Dundee Rights of Way Association claimed that it had not been consulted. If there were to be a bridge it must include a public footpath.

The sustained clamour of disapproval set up vibrations of uneasiness among the supporters of the Undertaking. It became apparent to Cox and to Lawyer Thornton that most of them would defect at the slightest pressure. Thornton called another meeting at which it was agreed to withdraw their skirmishing line and entrench. The Bill fell through.

The North British, realizing that it must now make some positive move or see the whole idea of a bridge lost, agreed to promote its own bridge. Thomas Bouch, working very hard through the winter of 1864–5, changed his plans and deposited new designs for a bridge 300 yards west of the original one. He proposed a ribbon of iron reaching out from Wormit Bay on the south bank to a point west of the Binns of Blackness. From there the line was to be carried to the high ground over the Dundee and Perth Railway, curving and reaching eastward to the west flank of the city.

The second Bill was to come before Parliament in the session of 1865–6.

The Caledonian seemed to experience a change of heart. Its directors met the directors of the North British and worked out their joint financial responsibility once the North British line crossed the Tay. The Caledonian could afford to be this magnanimous. If the river was going to be bridged they felt it essential to protect their rights and privileges. Meanwhile they continued to take steps to make sure that this Bill too would be withdrawn.

They took over the Scottish North Eastern and they transferred their lobbying to the House of Commons. They knew that the North British, impoverished, unsettled by dissension, would break down if the opposition in the House was strong enough. They based their opposition on the fact that the North British could not afford to pay for the bridge.

And indeed when the North British loosened its purse-strings it found that this was so. It withdrew its Bill.

Now the Caledonian, with the smile of a tiger, talked peace with the North British, and suggested an armistice in the bitter price war. But the Caledonian had won a great victory, and in industry there is no compassion for the vanquished. Mr Eborall again listened to complaints from the North British, and made his decisions honestly and impartially but without much hope of getting these two wild animals in harmony.

Patrick Matthew looked at his apples and smiled, and was pleased that there was no more talk about this terrible and dangerous bridge. A man who had been born in the eighteenth century could not be expected to enjoy the harsh vision of the twentieth century confronting him on his death-bed.

At the moment of its defeat, however, the Undertaking received the support of the one man who was to drive it through to success.

In November, 1866, a few months after the Bill foundered, John Stirling of Kippendavie became chairman of the North British Railway. In an industry that was dominated by such picaresque characters as George Hudson he was a man of unusual breeding and gentility. He had become Laird of Kippendavie and Lord of Kippenross before he was ten years old, and although he was rich enough to grow and enjoy a life of rustic leisure, his astute and agile mind drove him into railway politics.

He became one of the most powerful men in the Scottish North Eastern Railway, and he struck a hard bargain with the Caledonian when that octopus took over the line. Perhaps the cruel nature of the struggle that preceded the surrender left him with a gentlemanly distaste for the tactics and behaviour of the big company. Certainly when he became chairman of the North British he was determined to break the Caledonian's hold on Scotland.

Moribund, frightened though it was, the North British was the only other company that could do this, and the Tay Bridge would be its only successful weapon.

Stirling was fifty-five, and he had been engaged in the long, atrophying warfare of railway politics for the whole of his adult life. He was at an age when most men would have been content to let their life unreel itself in its own way, with the least entanglement.

But Stirling chose to fight for the Tay Bridge. Perhaps he knew that, for all its breast-beating, the heart was going out of the Caledonian. The bridge was inevitable. It would be built. The Caledonian could not stop it, it could only halt it.

Stirling let it be known in Dundee that the North British Rail-way was once more ready to consider the Undertaking.

So once again the supporters of the scheme met, in the Council Room at Dundee on 7 September 1869. There was James Cox, now a Baillie, there was Lawyer Thornton, and there was a representative sprinkling of Councillors and Harbour Trustees. There was Thomas Bouch, the uncommon denominator of them all.

Stirling spoke to them amiably, suggesting that he thought there would be little difficulty in bringing his company behind the Undertaking. With what must have been an ironical smile he referred to the one factor that should convince the most violent of opponents among his shareholders. The North British Railway was paying £9,000 a year for the use of the short stretch of railway between Broughty Ferry and Dundee. The building of a bridge would save the North British this money.

His directors, he said, would recommend the company to guarantee 5¼ per cent on the stock in the Undertaking.

The meeting ended in expressions of mutual goodwill, and Thomas Bouch took the Tay Ferry, and took the Fife train, and then took the Forth Ferry to Edinburgh, his strangely remote spirit uplifted.

But when Stirling called a meeting of North British share-holders they received him uneasily. They said his proposal was an outright declaration of war on the Caledonian.

'We are not declaring war . . .' said Stirling gently, but he and his board, and every shareholder in the room, knew that they were. Once the North British secured a foothold across the Tay it would carry much of the passenger and goods traffic now wholly carried by the Caledonian or its allies.

Exactly, said Stirling. But was that not why they *must* build the bridge? Without it and the trade it would bring the North British would die.

For how much?

For, perhaps, £250,000.

'Build it for that and I am content,' said one shareholder, 'and the sooner the better. But it is in my mind that it will cost double that sum.' To emphasize what he meant, he voted against the proposal.

But Stirling carried the majority with him, which he must have done as much by force of personality as by argument. Perhaps, in his own long struggle with the Caledonian, he had discovered that company's breaking-point, and knew that it would be the bridge.

Certainly the Caledonian almost crippled itself in a last attempt to destroy the North British, cutting goods rates and passenger fares still further. Out on the roads plate-laying gangs of the rival companies, Irishmen for the most part, came to blows and on one occasion to murder. Booking-clerks flailed their fists on Waverley station and disgusted a public who now did not care which railway controlled Scotland, so long as it meant that they would be able to travel in carriages that were well-furnished, well-heated, and well-ventilated, something which could not be said for the North British stock.

In the year 1869, the North British Railway Company came as close to collapse as it had ever been.

'We have three hundred stations,' said Stirling bluntly, 'yet our traffic per mile is £1,058, while the Caledonian, with fewer lines and fewer stations, is £1,458.'

Survival rested on the bridge, the rainbow bridge of Thomas Bouch.

Stirling realized that the opposition was weakening. Although it was noisy it was not strong enough to defeat the new Bill in Parliament. He was sure of this when the Tay Navigation Commissioners travelled down to Edinburgh to see him. Speaking for Perth, they said they now had no objection to the bridge, provided its central girders were a hundred feet from the water, high enough to permit the passage of sea-going ships. Stirling smiled, and charmed them, exacting from them a promise of no further opposition should he make the bridge as high as they wished.

The City of Perth needed much charming. Its dignity had been injured by the ribald humour of the Dundee Press which had described it as 'a rest-and-be thankful spot, whose fleet upon the Tay consists chiefly of some sand-sloops, not so large as Tyne wherries.'

Bouch needed charming, too. He knew that the truck of the largest ship likely to go up-river was not more than 70 feet from the water, and consequently his designs had allowed for a clearance of no more than 80 feet. But Stirling talked him into making the figure 100. Bouch was too busy that year to argue much. He was worrying about the river-bed. He had commissioned 'a thoroughly experienced borer, Mr Wylie' to take soundings from bank to bank. Mr Wylie did so, and reported the happy news that there was solid rock foundations all the way across, with the exception of some 250 yards on the north shore. His figures were accepted, which later proved most unfortunate.

Stirling's charm was needed again when the Dundee Harbour Trustees, under Provost Yeaman, received their copy of the new North British Bill. They read the small print and were horrified to discover two clauses sanctioning a subscription of £50,000 on their part. Yeaman set off for Edinburgh to tell Stirling that someone had 'acted most impertinently.' It was true that the Harbour Trustees were no longer placing any obstacle in the way of the bridge, but that did not mean they were putting all this money behind it. Stirling politely withdrew the clauses, and Provost Yeaman left with a lasting admiration for the railway laird.

In the last week of March 1870, the North British defended its Bill before Committee in the House of Commons. Its opponents, the only opponents left now, were the Tay Navigation Commissioners and the Caledonian Railway. The men from Perth were making a token opposition only, Stirling having bought them off with his promise of the High Girders. The Caledonian, left thus isolated, facing the charge of deliberately halting the natural progress of the industry, declared no opposition to the bridge in principle, but reserved doubts about the financial strength of its proposers.

Had the public not grown enthusiastic about the bridge the Caledonian's lobbying might have had stronger effect than it did. Stirling, now know affectionately as 'old Kippen Davie,' hurried from Westminster to a half-yearly meeting of his company. There, peering amiably in his myopia, he frightened the shareholders with the dark prospect of a future without the bridge, argued down opposition by showing that it came largely from those men who had also held shares in the Caledonian, and finally talked the meeting into subscribing another £10,000 to the Tay Bridge Undertaking.

The idea of bridging the wide estuary of the Tay had caught the imagination of the nation. The originality of this proposal to weave iron and masonry through two miles of air and water pleased people who had accepted the notion that all that was new in this century of scientific endeavour would be done by Britain. It was an age of new gods, and although the British people were resentful of the ignorant superstitions of lesser races they were civilizing, they saw no paradox in the blind trust they placed in their own industrial witch-doctors.

The country had implicit faith in Mr Bouch, a matter which, after some twenty years of hawking his dream, may have seemed odd to him. If he thought of it at all.

Meanwhile, spending his last summer on earth, Patrick Matthew was still in good voice. He said 'The scheme of the North British Railway to get Dundee capitalists to make a bridge for them in order to raise their drooping shares, is not succeeding to their wish.'

It was, of course, but this inaccuracy was merely the old man's preamble to far more accurate prophecy.

'The foundations of the piers will, we may expect, be very unequal, very unsafe, or very costly; some of them standing firm as the rock itself, others are as false as the foundations of the Royal Exchange.'

Correspondents signing themselves 'Disinterested Gentlemen,' which meant that they wished all to know they had no financial interest in the railway company or the Undertaking, pointed out to the apple-grower that one should move with the times, that Britain was under obligation to the rest of the world to point a way, and occasionally that it was God's will to bridge the Tay.

The clichés read well, but they merely exasperated the Seer of Gourdie. When he was reminded of the iron ship *Great Eastern*, he exploded with ridicule.

'The *Great Eastern* was just another blunder as the erection of this great bridge will be. They are both steps wide of precedent and beyond experience.'

Nor was he kind about the Houses of Parliament, newly pricking Westminster with their Gothic pinnacles. The man who suggested they proved Britain's power to build anything was patently a fool.

'The wretched, mouldering state of the recently-erected Houses of Parliament shows how stupid or careless some of our foremost masonic engineers can be.'

His anger increased as the Bill went before the House. 'How can Parliament know anything about bridges?'

How could an apple-grower, for that matter? But he did not say.

'The gross ignorance of both Parliament and its engineers has been exemplified in the wretched failure of their own new House, already crumbling to dust.'

On 15 July 1870 the Bill received the Royal Assent. The Kingdom of Fife was to be an island no longer. Engineers in Europe and America waited curiously to see what this bridge would be. Nowhere else in the world was there anything like it. The responsibility that rested on Bouch's shoulders was tremendous, but if it moved him to doubt, or to humility, or even to fear, he put none of these secret feelings into words.

Why should he? He had lived with his dream for twenty years, and this was too long for fears or doubts to survive. Only the stubborn determination now remained. Every bridge he had built had, in one way or another, tested and tried some feature he proposed to put into his bridge across the Tay. He had faith in it that did not burn or flare, but smouldered imperceptibly as he became busy at his drawing-board that summer and autumn.

These were fine weeks along the Tay, rich in sunshine and colour. People could scarcely remember such weather. But with September (as the North British once more declared no Ordinary dividend) strong winds began to blow down from the Ochils, picking tiles and chimney-cairns from Dundee roofs, and, among others, plucking out the fragile life of Patrick Matthew of Gourdiehill.

He died fighting, of course. He looked into the future and saw the bridge built, this rainbow bridge, this ribbon of iron. He saw a great wind wrenching at the High Girders, crushing the bridge. It was too terrible a vision, his last vision. He wrote hurriedly.

'In the case of accident with a heavy passenger train on the bridge the whole of the passengers will be killed. The eels will come to gloat over in delight the horrible wreck and banquet.'

Then the old man died, and left the bridge to its designer and its builders, and to the Great Storm of 28 December 1879.

# III

## 'A very long bridge,' said General Grant

THE Reverend Mr Thomson, Minister of Forgan, was appointed, or appointed himself, or became by the simple accident of his parish, the chaplain to the Tay Bridge Undertaking. He prayed mightily in its favour for seven years, and may have asked himself later what went wrong with his prayers.

What words he used to ask the Almighty's blessing when the foundation stone was laid on the south bank we do not know, for Mr Bouch had made it plain to the contractors, and to the directors of the Undertaking, that he would not have the gentlemen of the Press within earshot of Wormit. It was Saturday, 22 July 1871, a day of good sunlight, with a stiffish breeze coming down the firth, and Thomas Bouch stood there, holding his hat, and perhaps not caring that it was not his son, but another man's who gave the three orthodox knocks to the stone.

It was a boy called Paterson, son to William Paterson, Resident Engineer of the North British Railway, who stood behind the stone with mason's hammer in hand, while Mr Thomson uttered those words by which men enlist the sympathy of God in their wars or their business undertakings.

There were few spectators. The little wind-blown group stood high on the promontory above Wormit, and to the north of them stretched the terribly wide run of the estuary, smooth and deceptively calm. A mile, a mile and a quarter away the sun sparked on the windows of Dundee, and mellowed the girdle of smoke about Dundee Law. To the north-west was the blue-green fold of the Sidlaws, the flat Carse of Gowrie below which, in some kirkyard, Patrick Matthew lay at rest, and at last in silence.

A handful of workmen stood at a discreet distance while the

gentlemen went through the little ceremony. It was, if anything, to be their bridge, whoever had designed it and contracted for it and paid for it. When all the agreements were
made, men still had to go out there on to the river and work
against the persistent four-miles-an-hour tug of the tide, to
burrow twenty feet or more into the riverbed, to work in hot
caissons by the light of a half-penny candle, to die some of them,
and to suffer it all for eightpence an hour. But they knew it
would be a steady job for three years, Mr Bouch had so prom-
ised, and they lifted their bonnets and cheered when Sheriff
Monro of Kinross and Clackmannan proposed success to the
Undertaking in a few appropriate words.

Then the gentlemen took a dram, and the workmen took beer
supplied them by Mr Albert Groethe on behalf of the contractors, and Mr Thomson went back to his manse, the Sheriff
went back to Kinross, and Mr Bouch went to Tayport, and there
was nothing more to do but build the bridge.

For the rest of the day the Union flag snapped and fluttered
above the foundation stone.

From shore to shore the river distance to be bridged was just
over a mile, but the bends necessary at either bank, the oblique
drive of the bridge across the river, increased this distance to all
but two miles. Bouch's plans, as they existed in July 1871, proposed a latticed girder bridge on tall brick piers, carrying a
single railway line. There were to be some eighty-five spans,
ranging in length from 28 feet to 285 feet.

For the centre of the bridge, and the happiness of the citizens
of Perth, he had designed fourteen central spans, 200 feet in
length, which were known as the High Girders, because
whereas on the other spans the rail-line ran along the top of the
box girders, it would pass *through* the raised central spans, thus
giving clearance for river shipping.

There had been few bids for the contract. There were not
many contractors who had either the experience or the facilities to undertake work of such magnitude. Even those who
thought they could build the bridge were held back by a belief
that it was impossible to bid for it with any accuracy. The first

tender to be accepted came from the firm of Butler and Pitts. Mr Pitts was the monied partner of the company, and when he died, shortly after the acceptance of the tender, the contract fell through.

In some musical compositions a single note, or a phrase, is struck early, and almost casually, in the first movement. It is often missed at the first hearing of the theme and mood of the whole work. Mr Pitts' unfortunate death might be considered as such an ominous note.

In May 1871, the North British Railway entered into a second contract, with Charles de Bergue & Co., of London, Cardiff, and Manchester, the price being £217,000, and the specified time for completion, three years. Neither figure was to prove an accurate estimate, or even a reasonable one.

Old Charles de Bergue, however, was one of the foremost contractors of the day, and a renowned figure in engineering. If there was anything odd about his behaviour nobody recognized it as incipient insanity.

The contractor's manager on the spot was Albert Groethe, a burly gentleman of German descent, with a passionless face and a generous heart, much given to writing about his work in *Good Words*, yet, withal, possessing an appreciation of labour-management relations unusual in his day. The foundation stone had scarcely been laid at Wormit when Groethe insisted on the formation of a Tay Bridge Co-operative Association for his workmen, and also a dining-hall, reading-room, kitchen, dormitories, and 'Victuals at a reasonable price.'

He was a popular figure in Dundee, and a good speaker. The unusual nature of his work projected his merits beyond their actual proportions, and he was much in demand for lectures to gentlemen's clubs, to meetings of the Young Men's Christian Association, to chapel socials, whereat he told as much about the building of the bridge as he could.

He was much amused by the thought that the bridge might be destroyed by a storm.

Seventy men and boys began to build the bridge. Most of them came from Fife and Forfar, although there were a few itinerant labourers from England and Ireland. These men worked twelve hours a day, and at no time did any of them receive more than tenpence an hour for their work. They had names like Ferguson, Macdonald, Macbeth, Stewart, Robertson, and McGowan. Their grandfathers had been Lowland farmers, Highland crofters, and when they sat in their bothies during the dour winter days, waiting for a half-gale to blow itself out, they sang songs and told stories that were part of the unwritten folk-lore of peasant Scotland. They had their feet in two worlds, the world of their grandfathers and the new world that was theirs, one of iron and cement and cherry-red rivets. If the weed-green stumps that jut from the Tay today are Thomas Bouch's un-happy memorial, they are an equally poignant reminder of the Scotsmen who built the first Tay Bridge, and whose names have slipped into the oblivion that awaits most of us.

The contractors had selected the south bank as the base of their operations. It was the plain, sensible choice. On the north shore the land ran down to the river and broke into sandy shelves below Magdalen Green, but on the south, at Wormit, a series of trap rocks rose precipitously, fifty feet above high water mark. From here the bridge would take its great leap.

There was no shore below the rocks, of course, but that could be built, first a wharf eighty yards out into the Tay on which materials could be landed, and then wooden staging for the girders.

But it was necessary to have land on the point for the erec-tion of offices, workshops, and those dormitories of Albert Groethe's. The Laird of Birkhill, one Wedderburn, whose land this was, was reluctant to sell it, and even petitioned the Court of Sessions to prevent the Undertaking from buying it. He did not want anything built on his land, even a privy. The argu-ments for and against were debated before Lord Mackenzie, who finally rejected the Laird of Birkhill's petition.

By the middle of September the land abutment had been com-pleted, 'a most substantial piece of masonry' according to those who made the uncomfortable autumn journey across the river by ferry to see how the great work was coming along. It was made from huge blocks of stone quarried at Carmyle. Two piers were already completed and a third was in progress, rectangular columns thrusting up from the water, built wholly of brick and set in Portland cement.

So that there might be no need for water scaffolding, these monoliths had been built on shore and floated out to their position by barge, from a section of the beach that had been levelled and laid with a floor of cement.

In the beginning the piers were built in two parts, two cylinders of wrought iron filled with a lining of brickwork up to the level of low water, with an opening in the centre. They were carried out on two pontoons and sunk to their positions on the river-bed. Each cylinder weighed 40 tons, which was formidable, but toylike compared with those that were to be built later. Once the cylinders rested uneasily on the bed of the river the water was sucked out of them.

Then came a nightmare of candle-licked darkness and danger. Caisson gangs were lowered into the cylinders, down to the gravel at the bottom. In a space no more than nine and a half feet in diameter, men and boys dug with pick, spade and the claws of their hands, in freezing or roasting temperatures, and for as much as ten hours at a time, sending up the river-soil in baskets. As they dug the cylinder settled down about them until it rested firmly on the rock-shelf which, according to Mr Wylie, was there waiting all the way across the river.

Once the cylinder was made secure on the rock foundation, the base and shaft were filled with cement, so that it became a solid mass of brickwork and concrete encased in a cuirass of iron. The temporary caissons above water level were then removed, and the brickwork carried up to the required height of the pier.

Six piers were built out into the river by this method, until it was realized that the narrowness of the cylinders increased the difficulties. Often one side of a cylinder would rest on a boulder, while the other sank quickly into sand, and naked, sweating men fought to reach the top before the water rushed in, or the cylinder canted over and crushed them.

Groethe decided to construct the pier-bases as one complete structure, rather than two separate pillars. The tenth pier from Wormit was the first to be so constructed, consisting of two engaged cylindrical pillars rising from a common base, having long straight sides and circular ends. It was a tremendous achievement, and, after Mr Groethe had lectured upon it successfully, trippers came from Dundee and Tayport and Leuchars to stare at the work.

First, a wrought-iron base was built on the land abutment, 3 feet high, 22½ feet long, and 10½ feet wide, with flat sides and circular ends. It was laid on the concrete floor at the water's edge. It was then surrounded by a conical cast-iron structure 5 feet high, in which twelve men would work with ease, or what seemed like ease. The whole thing was unwieldy. It weighed 140 tons, and it was carried out to its position by two pontoons, each of which carried hydraulic rams capable of lifting 60 tons.

To see this gaunt, terrifying structure, moving out on to the river with a grim dignity, dwarfing the men that swarmed above and about it, reminded one observer of other stupendous achievements, such as the building of the great pyramids. He qualified the comparison, however, with the thought that here on the Tay was a monument to an enlightened age, constructed by free and happy labour, joyous in praise of the Lord.

Once the pontoons were anchored in position, the base was lowered into the water, its position being accurately judged by means of sighting lines to the shore, and by a measuring chain from the last pier. Wrought-iron caissons, like the pot-helmets of Ironside troopers, were fixed upon it and water was sucked out, and the half naked digging gangs went down with their candles and gouged out the gravel until the base sank to its rock foundation.

Thus the work went speedily, and there was no doubt that the bridge would be completed within three years.

Then, at the beginning of 1873, Mr de Bergue gave convincing and alarming proofs of his insanity. Before the month of April was out he had gone to join Mr Pitt.

Perhaps he had been the only member of his firm who had

wished to build the bridge, for his heirs went cap in hand to the
North British Railway and asked to be relieved of the contract.
It was three months before another contractor, Hopkins, Gilkes
& Co. Ltd, of Middlesbrough, took over the work and confirmed
Albert Groethe as their resident manager.

For thirty years this company had been building bridges of
iron, high bridges and low, and long and curving bridges, and it
had built many for Thomas Bouch, the Beelah viaduct for
example. Mr Edgar Gilkes was fortunately a sane man in good
health. He had much faith in himself, in his company, and in
the skill of Thomas Bouch. He was supported in this faith by
one of his principal shareholders, William Bouch, brother of
Thomas.

The new contractors put fresh impulse into the building.
They opened an iron foundry on the Wormit bank so that
girders might be cast on the spot, avoiding the long wait for
their delivery from England. At the time this seemed to be a
splendid idea, and so it might have proved to be had not everybody trusted a foreman called Ferguson who found, not entirely
to his distaste, that he was left in virtual charge of the whole
foundry.

Mad Mr de Bergue's sudden death was not the only awkward
development that hampered the bridge-builders that year.
Almost coincidently Thomas Bouch was informed that his
happy assumption of a rock-bed eighteen to twenty feet below
the gravel, and all the way across the river, was no more than an
assumption. Something had been wrong with Mr Wylie's
borings. It may have been the fact that although he was a competent mineral borer he had had no previous experience of
river-boring.

Shortly after the sinking of the tenth pier-base Groethe discovered that the rock-bed was now forty feet down in many
places, and in one sounding he went 157 feet below the river-bed
and still did not find rock.

So over from the Continent came Gerrit Willem Camphuis
who, with a diploma from the Public Works Department of
Holland (but no previous experience of bridge-building), and

with a team of experienced pile-drivers, drove piles down towards that distant shelf of sandstone, constructing artificial rock-beds on which the piers might rest. But these piers could no longer be the solid, imposing brick columns that had marched boldly out into the Tay from the Wormit bank. Now Bouch designed iron columns to rest on a brick and concrete base, and span by span they were to add their delicate tracery to the whole impossible fragility of the rainbow bridge.

Bouch had been forced, by this river which he believed he knew better than his garden at Moffat, to amend his design once more. He put none of his disgust on paper, but sat down with his assistants, with the mathematical support of Mr Stewart, and drew his fresh plans, while the workmen waited and the summer drifted on towards another unhappy winter.

Two years had passed, and from the Dundee shore the bridge seemed scarcely begun. Keen eyes could see the thumb-like stumps of the piers of course, and there was now the glow and smoke-belch of the new foundries. The pulse-beat of the pile-drivers went on day and night. But in daylight, when the sun shone and the mists lifted, the Tay was still wide, and un-bridged.

Bouch made his emendations. The remaining piers were now to rest on wider bases, with superstructures of cylindrical cast-iron columns, strutted and cross-braced. These columns were in sections, bolted vertically through flanges, the whole appearing like the sort of complicated, useless strings of knitting that children sometimes make with a cotton-reel and half a dozen nails.

Along with these, Bouch made other changes. He altered the sequence of the spans. Instead of fourteen High Girders of 200-feet spans, there were now to be thirteen, eleven of 245 feet and two of 227 feet.

There were now to be *thirteen* High Girders, which may or may not prove something about unlucky numbers.

Work went on again in the autumn of 1873. All night the glow of the Wormit foundry was a scarlet blot on the southern horizon. During the day it was a cloud of smoke that occasion-ally burst into lazily floating sparks. Month after month, year after year, the air was now never quite free from a thumping and a ringing, and a high calling of voices, coming across the river, as the men of Fife and Forfar knitted their strand of iron from pier to pier.

But its progress was 'by no means as rapid as had been anticipated by the more sanguine shareholders who seemed to have expected to see the structure reared like a fabric in fairyland'. They grumbled and they whispered, and a few of them had second and frightened thoughts about the whole crazy idea. Bouch ignored them when they stopped him in the Royal Hotel, Dundee. He brushed them aside as they caught his sleeve, asking him for reassurance. Groethe, however, smiled, and was willing to spend his time comforting them, pouring into them some of his own ready confidence.

The girders were going up, linking pier to pier, and producing something that looked as if it might, given luck and God's grace, be a bridge one day.

Erecting the girders was a formidable task. Each span was built on the staging offshore, its ends projecting beyond the planking, with water below and enough clearance for a barge to float. A span for the High Girders, 245 feet in length, took four weeks to build, with over 18,000 rivets holding its struts and tie-bars. A monster of 190 tons.

Once it was completed, part of the staging was taken away, and barges were floated beneath either end. At high water the girder was taken out into the river and aligned between its piers. There eighty men, crawling upon it, worked the hydraulic jacks which slowly raised the span, 20 feet a day, until its ends were above the top of the piers. This point was reached always at turn of the tide, so that as the water fell and the barges dropped, the girder came down slowly until it rested on the pier-heads, and the workers climbed up and over it, bolting it firm, and filling the air with the clang of their hammers and the rich colour of their oaths.

Eighty men, 190 tons of cast-iron, hydraulic jacks and two barges, a river pulling at 4 miles an hour, a wind blowing at 30, heat, cold, rain and sleet, for tenpence an hour.

By April 1876 seventy-six of the eighty-five spans had been
built, and only eighteen girders were still needed to fill the gaps.
In the autumn of that year two electric lights were used to
speed the night work. They were large lamps with parabolic
reflectors, each with 'an illuminating power equal to 1,000
candles, the current generated by two of Gramme's electro-mag-
netic machines, driven by an engine of four horsepower'.

They stood on an eminence at Wormit, shining down on the
staging where the girders were building, and the glow of them
turned the Tay water to milk. People stood on Magdalen Green
in the evenings to look silently at a marvel that would be com-
monplace to their grandchildren.

So it was becoming a bridge after all, and a marvel of the
world which men must see.

By a trick of the eye its slenderness seemed to emphasize the
vast grandeur of the Tay basin, the broad river's yellow face,
the saucer-rim of the blue hills, spreading reaches against which
the iron bridge appeared to be an impertinent cotton thread
spun from matchstick to matchstick. At week-ends the people
of Dundee would take the ferry to Newport to wonder at the
bridge banding the river to the west. And from Newport they
took carriages to Wormit for a closer view of the iron and brick,
to be thrilled by the acrid scent of hot iron at the foundries, the
sweet smell of sawdust, and to watch the sea-birds wheel and
settle on the girders.

There were other visits, professional visits, deputations from
the Cleveland Institute of Engineers, from the Institution of Engineers and Shipbuilders in Scotland, and such men came to ask
questions, and to take notes against future lectures. The directors and shareholders of the Undertaking also made frequent
visits to satisfy their own or their wives' curiosity, to walk
southward into the green Fifeshire hills and see the railway
line that was being cut there.

During one such visit ex-Baillie Yeaman, now an M.P., went
down a caisson into the wet, candle-lit darkness, and came up
expressing himself much intrigued by the manner in which the
good workmen were digging out the river-bed.

There was also 'Captain Wentzel of the Royal Horse Guards of the King of Holland', who visited the bridge and took part in a jolly evening in the workmen's dining-hall. There was the sad old Emperor of Brazil, who thought that the mouth of the Amazon could do with such a bridge too. There was Prince Leopold, who came over for a visit while staying with the Governor of Fifeshire. He came in September 1877, when the bridge was nearly completed. He drove up to Newport in a fine carriage, raising his hat politely to all who recognized him, and he took the ferry across to Dundee in the company of Mr Bouch, asking pertinent and polite questions about the design and the construction.

He drove to Magdalen Green in the centre of a civic party, and the crowd cheered with delight as the young Prince ran smartly up the steps to the bridge. There, on a temporary line, was waiting a panting ballast engine, and behind it a wagon, draped with crimson cloth. The Prince and Mr Bouch took their seats in this and were taken out to the fourth great girder from the northern bank, where the Prince got out, took off his hat and let the wind blow his hair about his face as he said to Mr Bouch that he admired not only 'the elegance of the structure, but its solid substantiality'.

But the visit which the people of Dundee and the builders of the bridge enjoyed most was that made by General Ulysses Simpson Grant, ex-President of the United States. He was in England with his wife, and his youngest son Jesse, and in the autumn of 1877 was making his way northward, seeing many things, attending many congratulatory luncheons and dinners, and listening to many and the same expressions of admiration for his military genius. By the time he reached Dundee he appears to have been somewhat tired of the whole thing, and would have infinitely preferred to be at home with a good glass and a strong stogie.

He came up from Edinburgh in a special train on 1 September 1877, with the Lord Provost of Edinburgh, Sir James Falshaw, Mr and Mrs Bouch, and as many ladies and gentlemen who could find seats on the train.

Grant is a good Scots name, and the people of Scotland were happy that a man with a good Scots name had not only won the American Civil War, but had become President of the United States as well. They flooded out to line the rails all the way through Fifeshire, cheering as soon as they caught sight of a blunt, bearded face scowling down at them from the window of a claret-coloured coach.

On the platform at Tayport, awaiting the special, ex-Provost Cox, and Edgar Gilkes, and the rest of the reception committee fretted impatiently, looking at the non-committal sky and wondering which of their plans should be put into operation – the one for fair weather or the one for foul. The day turned out to be neither, but since it did not rain they decided to go ahead as if the sun were shining.

The train drew into Tayport at 11.35 a.m., and General Grant got out, stretched his short legs, shook hands briskly, nodded, and let Mrs Grant do most of the talking. This she did extremely well.

In Tayport harbour the tug *Excelsior* was waiting to carry the party over the river. Close by the tug's wheel, nominally if not nautically in command of her, Albert Groethe dominated the little vessel.

There was a great crowd on the quayside, ringed by a cordon of police whose intervention 'was at no period necessary, the crowd, while manifesting a pardonable anxiety to see the General, never overstepped the bounds of decorum'. This seems to have gratified Grant's military eye, for he took off his hat, grinned and waved, until Mrs Grant took his arm.

At noon Old Glory was unbent at the *Excelsior*'s mast-head, and it flew also from every window on shore, garlanded with heather. There was red, white and blue bunting up and down the river, from the lighthouses to the bridge, and a Mr Harry Walsh of Tayport risked his life as he leant from his window to wave the Stars and Stripes, the better to emphasize his admiration for the little Union soldier.

On the quay two bands competed against each other in *The Battle Hymn of the Republic*.

Grant was told that the *Excelsior* would make a cursory tour of the bridge, after which there would be a civic lunch. But both he and the reception committee reckoned without the enthusiasm of Mr Thomas Knox. Knox was secretary of the Edinburgh branch of the *Mars* Institution, a philanthropic organization which ran the training-ship *Mars* off the Dundee foreshore, where orphan boys were trained for service with the Navy, the Army, and the Merchant Marine.

Knox had somehow got himself aboard the *Excelsior* where 'his enthusiastic advocacy overcame any scruples that the General may have had'. From the General's point of view a visit to the bridge, a visit to a training-ship, what did it matter, so long as the lunch was good, and soon?

So the *Excelsior* altered course to lay alongside the *Mars*, where the boys were already lining the yards, and were drawn up on deck to give hearty cheers as the tug steamed by. When the *Excelsior* made signal that the General was in fact coming aboard, Captain Scott, Master of the *Mars*, did his best. He ordered the band to strike up the German War Song.

A grey spade-beard jutted over the quarter-deck taffrail, pulled a tubby little body after it, and the whole waited patiently until the band blew itself into silence. The victor of Vicksburg said nothing, while everybody else was explaining to him the purpose of the *Mars*, the integrity of the boys, and the excellence of their training. There was then a silence, until an officer of the ship gestured to the boy's choir, which immediately began to sing *Alouette*. Before the last stanza was reached, a second officer rang the fire-bell, and the little fellows scampered this way and that about the General's legs while he stood nodding his approval jerkily.

Captain Scott was at his elbow, thanking him for the honour, assuring him that it would be long remembered, longer even, if the General could think of a few words to say to the boys. He could not (there was no sign of lunch yet), and he looked sideways at Sir James Falshaw, who stepped forward.

'Boys! Here is a great general come to see you, and I am sure what he would say to you would be – Obedience, Attention to those above you, fulfil all the duties incumbent upon you. You must all strive to rise to be great men and useful members of society.'

Here ex-Provost James Cox interrupted. 'There may be generals among *you*, boys.'

'Well,' said Sir James, considering this an ambition as much above the boys' powers as their rights, 'there will be many corporals among you, at least.'

Then three more piping cheers and the General returned to the *Excelsior*, which was at last pointed to the bridge. Once there it turned north, and, with the tall piers stretching above it, cruised up and down while Mr Groethe explained the method of construction, the difficulties encountered and overcome, and the General nodded curtly to it all and said 'I understand!' several times, until Mr Gilkes said that it was now time to go ashore for lunch.

Lunch was a small affair in the offices of the Undertaking, with James Cox presiding at the General's table, and Mr Gilkes at his lady's. But lunch, which was excellent, had to be paid for by speeches, through which the General sat glumly. A certain schoolboy jolliness characterized the long speeches, with Mr Gilkes saying that there was no point in apologizing for the smallness of the room in which they lunched, that wouldn't make it larger. He proposed the health of General and Mrs Grant.

Grant stood up. 'Gentlemen! Inasmuch as you have coupled Mrs Grant's name with mine I think it is only fair to call upon her to respond.'

There was laughter, and nobody (except perhaps Mrs Grant) took the suggestion seriously. So the General thanked everybody and sat down.

And for an hour or more he sat there while the directors and members of the Tay Bridge Undertaking bathed luxuriously in mutual admiration, proposing this health and that until finally they remembered the man who was responsible for their presence, the General's presence, the bridge itself. The call was for 'Mr Bouch!'

Albert Groethe raised his hand. 'Mr Bouch,' he said, 'wishes me to return thanks for the toast. Mr Bouch considered there is not room enough for him here. There is much more outside today.'

At last lunch was over and carriages were called. There was a smart, hoof-clopping ride to Magdalen Green 'with a short stop at the Royal Hotel for the convenience of the ladies', during which the General stood on the pavement, smoking a cigar and nodding as passers-by raised their hats. At Magdalen Green he was asked if he would care to walk out along the bridge. He had no choice. He stumped along silently while the wind pulled at his coat and his thin hair, his eyes fixed on the back of the bunting-draped wagon ahead which was carrying the ladies to the last girder. Half a mile from the shore, and almost a mile from the point where they had ascended the bridge, and surely with his little legs exhausted, Grant listened to another speech, this time from Gilkes, who presented an album of Mr Valentine's photographs, showing the bridge in all stages of construction.

Then the walk back, with the wagon following now, and the ladies holding their hats with chilling hands. The General walked silently, clutching the red leather album beneath his arm. Just as silently he got into his carriage and was driven to the docks where the *Excelsior* was waiting with steam up. Dundee saw the last of the man as the tug turned its creamy bow-wave southwards and the water boiled beneath its counter. A little black figure beneath his country's flag, hat raised stiffly in salute.

When he was gone the directors tried to remember what it was the General had said out there on the bridge, his answer to Mr Gilkes' speech, his response to an inquiry about the sensations he must be feeling. Someone at last recalled the words.

'It is a very long bridge,' the General had said.

# IV

*'Life is not lost which is spent or sacrificed in
the grand enterprises of useful industry'*

I T was built against the resentment of the river and the wind.
Every hour the tidal flow tugged at the great caissons. The river-
bed quixotically and perversely changed its nature, now there
were great boulders that tore the nails from the fingers of the
diggers, or now sudden quicksands trapped men's feet in ugly
darkness and sucked them down to the waist. Every fourteen
days during the winter, and often as frequently in summer, a
full gale came down from the Central Highlands without warning, singing its derision along the half-complete girders. Waves
climbed as high as the pier-tops, and now and then licked a
workman from his hold there. Passengers on the Newport
ferries looked up from their sickness to stare at the iron band
and be thankful that it was not their duty to be building it,
though it was the greatest thing in the world.

From the beginning there was a struggle between the skill of
Albert Groethe, the courage of his workmen, and the ruthlessness of the river. He chose his words and his phrases
stylishly when he wrote of his work in *Good Words*, but sometimes his exasperation and his feeling of impotence came
through pathetically.

'Without any barometrical warning the storm came down at
four o'clock in the afternoon with unparalleled suddenness. No
gradual growth, no preliminary showers heralded its approach.
It was just high-water, and a very high spring tide it was . . .'

His diary showed that often there could be no more than five
or six favourable working days in a month. If the men on the
piers could not work, then the men erecting the girders on
shore, the men in the foundry, could not work either. The river

brought them all to a halt, and kept them at a halt until it had exhausted its anger.

Such delays sent the directors of the Undertaking to Parliament, where they successfully pleaded the viciousness of the weather and were granted more time, and still more time to finish the longest bridge in the world.

Within a month of Master Paterson's proud taps on the foundation stone a storm blew up suddenly from the southern spur of the Sidlaws, whipping along the Wormit shore, smashing huts, disabling barges, washing the wreckage of the half-completed staging downriver to the flats at Buddon Ness. In 1872 a single gale blew for three weeks without stay, something strange even in the Firth of Tay, and for three weeks it hid the erected piers in a veil of spray. The winter of 1874 was a bad winter. Sheep and men died on the hills, frozen into attitudes of incredulous astonishment, and the whole of Scotland from Sutherland to the Border was white and smooth under cruel snow. No work was done on the bridge. The workmen's braziers glowed in the bothies. Ice-floes, twelve inches thick and many feet across, leaped from the run of the river, and when they were gone after too many days Groethe went out in a tug, travelling from pier to pier until he was satisfied that they had done no damage.

Men died, crushed or drowned. One moment a man would be fly-perched upon a rising girder-span, and the next moment the wind had picked him off and flung him down eighty feet to the water. When Number 14 pier was being filled with cement the escape cock for the air became choked, and the pressure, normally 12 to 20lb. a square inch, rose and blew out a plate, so that the air-bell, and the engine that operated it, fell to a barge and crushed two men standing there.

The collapse of three cylinders on the south bank took two workmen into the mud, and held them there under the water until they drowned.

In August 1876, a barge carrying a span out to the High Girders, rocked uncertainly in a rising squall, broke away and began to drift towards the estuary mouth. The men aboard the barge put the girder end-on to the wind to retard the drift, but barge and girder swung and swung, until both were spinning giddily, as a leaf will rotate on its passage downstream. The crew of a steamer, which had been called upon for help, panicked as the swinging iron grazed across their stern. The ropes they flung, and which were made fast to the barge, snapped one by one, and the barge and girder drifted away into the darkness until at last they were caught and held by two tugs, and safely beached.

The men who built the Tay Bridge loved it because they were building it, but they knew that it was merciless, that it was iron and stone and without compassion for them.

At 2.30 a.m., on Tuesday, 26 August 1873, it killed six of them.

Pier 54, a quarter of a mile from Magdalen Green on the north bank, had been floated out some days before. The base rested on the river-bed, but had yet to be sunk to its permanent foundation. Below, in semi-darkness, in a hot, almost airless space 20 feet in diameter and only 8 feet high, the digging gangs worked the hours of day and night, scooping out sand and gravel. Above them was the air-bell, and the pumps drinking up the water. Men and boys worked in the candle-light and emerged to suck in fresh air, and drink a can of tea before going down again.

At five p.m. on Monday, 25 August a new gang went out to the pier for the night's work. There was William Johnston, the middle-aged foreman, and there was a boy of sixteen called William White. The others were James Gellately, Alexander Clelland, John Denholm, James Herd, William Stewart, Charles Thomson, A. Farquhar, and G. Anderson.

They worked through the early night hours. Above them, on the river surface, the weather was dark and surly and there was no moon. Thunder was rolling off the Ochils in a muttering cannonade. Now and then a whip of rain beat on the air-bell, on the face of William White standing there, and the wash of the tide slapped against the sides of the moored barges.

At 2.30 a.m. Foreman Johnston had just passed through the air-lock and was breathing in the sweet night-air. Below the lock, below in the base, Farquhar and Thomson were 'claying', stopping leakages with handslaps of wet clay. Anderson was on duty at the engine with the boy White. On the extreme bottom of the caisson were Clelland, Denholm, Gellately, Herd and Stewart.

Afterwards, Johnston said he felt no explosion, just a sudden rush of air as he came out of the air-lock. Then there was noise, the crash and wrench of breaking equipment, the eerie whine of tearing iron.

The boy White was plucked from the engine and lifted into the darkness, falling in a gentle curve until he struck the water. Half-stunned, bewildered, he sank down until his training (he had been a boy aboard the *Mars*) overcame his fear and he began to fight. When his head broke the surface he could see nothing of the bridge or the sky, only the dark shape of a barge slapping the water a few yards away. He swam to it and clawed at its slimy sides with his hands, sucking in air and water, spitting, shaking his head. He swam the whole length of the barge and found no rope, nothing that he could grasp and haul himself aboard.

He left the barge and pushed into the darkness again. There his threshing hands hit the clinkers of a small boat, the *Fanny*, and he pulled himself inboard, and lay there with his legs still on the gunnels.

Anderson was no swimmer. The explosion had thrown him into the river too, and he fell heavily. He was wearing heavy boots, a belted jacket and a fisherman's jersey. They sucked up the water's weight quickly and took him down. When he came up he cried out '*Is onybody there?*'

A floating plank struck his head, and he sank again, and came up, a yard or so from the *Fanny*, crying still '*Is onybody there?*'

White heard the cry. With his hands he paddled the *Fanny* towards Anderson's face. It was five minutes before the boy succeeded in dragging the frightened, struggling man inboard. Then White sat in the *Fanny*'s stern and paddled her in circles, searching for other members of the gang, and finding none. The painter of the little boat was fast moored to one of the barges, and she went backwards and forwards in a fan across the dark water.

When White tired, he and Anderson lay down for two hours, while the water swirled and gurgled past them, and the gale blew itself out. Anderson was very sick. Grey dawn at last came up the estuary, first brushing in the outline of the bridge lightly, and then painting it in firmer, clearer strokes. They saw the top of the pier, and the air-bell blown out in jagged metal. Clinging there to the iron-work, his mouth opened in a call that could not be heard, was Foreman Johnston. They shouted to him, and shouted again until he heard 'Wha are the ithers?'

Johnston shook his head, pointed down, and called again. White paddled the *Fanny* in closer, and they heard Johnston shout that he could see Farquhar lying below him on the brick-work.

White stood up in the uneasy boat and threw the foreman a line. Cold, almost delirious, Johnston pulled the boat up to the pier and climbed down into her, and then the two men and the boy sat on the thwarts and looked at the broken pillar until the light grew stronger, and they saw their friend Herd now, lying at the top of the shaft, his head at an odd and disturbing angle because there was a bar of iron across his neck.

Afterwards they were not able to explain how they got the injured Farquhar from the brickwork, but somehow they did, and they released the *Fanny*'s painter and rowed her towards Magdalen Green. There they got word to Groethe, who came hurrying down from his lodgings, calling for a boat to take him out to Pier 54.

Now the morning light was strong, and the water of the Tay was slipping past the piers with scarcely a ripple, and there was no wind at all. This was always the moment of apologetic calm that followed the river's great anger, and in it the bridge looked strong and indestructible.

The men on the tug saw another body, lying at the top of the shaft too. It was James Gellately, and he was dead.

Groethe went sadly back to Dundee. He had seen the effect of the explosion on the pier, and he knew that none of the men inside the shaft could be alive. There was a Minister standing at Magdalen Point, the Reverend Mr Piper, brought like a corbie by the news of disaster. A good man, though, who wept as he hurried away, at Grothe's request, to inform the wives of the dead men.

Later that morning an inspection party, headed by Groethe, went out and climbed the shaft. Muddy, evil water was slopping inside it. Within the airbell was a wash of wet sand and the body of Thomson. His neck was broken, and most of his bones, too, so that his limbs lay as if they were sleeves full of sawdust.

Since the other men must be below water, Grothe went back to Dundee and asked the Harbour Board for two divers. These men were Peter Harley and Charles Tate, experienced, phlegmatic men who were to dive and dive again at the bridge in five years' time. They went out that afternoon, in their inflated suits and great, metal helmets.

They found Stewart. He was lying on his back in the mud, legs and arms stretched in cruciform. There was blood on his face, and Harley washed this away with a movement of his hand. It was seen that Stewart's expression was calm and serene.

Nearby, a pair of feet, soles uppermost, projected from the mud. Harley and Tate dug with their hands, darkening the water as the sand swirled up. There was Clelland, and his face was neither calm nor serene.

Denholm was easily found. He was clinging to the lower spars of the ladder, one foot raised, and he looked as if with an effort he might yet climb, except that he was dead, too. His lips were drawn back over his teeth by the anguish of his long-past thoughts.

There was no clue to the cause of the explosion. The gauges showed a pressure of 14 lb. Not frequently the pressure had gone up to 20 lb., so this reading told Groethe nothing. It was generally believed that the plates could take a pressure as high as 50 lb. Groethe thought, and he said that it was his belief, that a coal barge, moored near the pier, had been flung against the caisson by the river, cracking a plate. But there was no way of proving this.

Four tiers of casting had been displaced on one side, and there was an aperture 8 feet across and 9 feet high through which sand and water had poured rapidly, trapping the six men below or driving some to the top as it killed them.

Groethe's honest feeling of responsibility towards his men was profoundly distressed. He called them to a meeting in the dining-room at Wormit. They stood or sat, with their bonnets slanting on their heads, clay pipes in their mouths, and they listened to him. He said that from that day forward no shift would work on the river bed for longer than eight hours.

They called out to him that it had been at their wish that they had worked twelve hours, and this they did not want changed. He knew that they were thinking of the money, but he said that his order must stand. There would be no shift longer than eight hours. He would, however, increase the top rate from eight-pence to tenpence an hour.

So they accepted his ruling and went back to work.

It was the Victorian age, and life and death had Purpose. There could be no disaster without a moral. Writing to the *Dundee Advertiser* a gentleman of Fifeshire discovered such a moral: 'Life is not lost which is spent or sacrificed in the grand enterprises of useful industry.'

A small collection was made for the widows and dependents of the dead.

There was a second major accident in February 1877, which, although less costly in life, did far more damage to the bridge. For some weeks building had been proceeding at a sharp and satisfactory rate. It was winter, but the weather had been gentle, the river agreeable. Now the thread was beginning to look like a bridge, with all the piers sunk, and almost all the spans in position. From the high ground at Lochee, on the north bank, it still looked an absurdly fragile thing, a lazily bending line across the firth, not straight even, but rising and falling in a graceful switchback.

The river-gangs were working on the High Girders. The south-ernmost two spans had been floated out on pontoons, and by Friday, 2 February had been raised by the hydraulic jacks ready to be lowered on to the pier-heads. They hung on strong steel pins, supported by temporary columns, 5 feet above the pier-heads. About forty men were working on them as the day drifted to dusk at 4 p.m.

There had been surly gusts of rain all day, but no sign of squalls. At times there was scarcely any wind. Just before dusk Groethe looked from his office window to the west. Three miles away, over Cartagena Bank, river-water and sky had between them produced one black grey cloud, poised and motionless. Groethe found this phenomenon disturbing. He studied it at length and then looked at the glass. It was steady. As he watched, the wind began to tease the southern end of the cloud, pulling it out into strands of wool.

Five minutes later the cloud grew suddenly to embrace the whole horizon, and began to move down the estuary at great speed. The glass in Groethe's office had dropped an inch. He ran out, leaving the door open, and the rising wind roughly fingered his deserted papers. He ran down to the jetty, shouting at the workmen to secure everything possible. But now the southern wing of the cloud brushed along the Wormit bank and was upon the bridge. A pontoon broke loose from the staging as the river heaved up to join the wind. The hawsers snapped, and the pontoon swung angrily into the river and went down-stream into the growing darkness.

Although spans 12 and 13 of the High Girders were not yet thoroughly secured, Groethe had no doubt that they would hold on the pins until the squall had blown itself out. But he was worried by the thought of the men out there, and he hailed Captain White of the *Excelsior*, and asked him to go out to the river with all speed, and bring the men in.

The Captain pointed up to the weather and shook his head. It was five o'clock, and the wind was coming out of the south-west at gale force now, in sudden angry punches. Desperate for the safety of his men as he was, Groethe had to admit that the *Excelsior* could not be risked in the storm.

The darkness was now thick, and if it hid the sight of the river and the bridge from the men on the banks, their imagination filled it with unpleasant pictures. By seven-thirty the

gale had in no way lessened, and White made the courageous
decision to take the *Excelsior* out. Privately he thought that the
wind must by now have blown every man from the girders, but
he steamed to within a hundred yards of the central spans,
with the *Excelsior* rising, pitching, falling and rolling in the
heavy water. He could see nothing. His navigation lights floated
scarlet and green on the waves, broken into a hundred reflec-
tions, but beyond them he could see nothing. He waited.

At a quarter past eight he and his crew heard three distinct
sounds, like the explosions of heavy cannon. Then a grinding,
screaming noise of agonized metal, followed by a tremendous
splash. A second or two later a great wave of water hit the
*Excelsior* on her starboard side and nearly capsized her. Floating
planks thudded along her sides, and White turned her down-
stream to escape them. Then he turned her back.

Hail was now falling, ringing in sharp, pretty notes on the
*Excelsior's* stack.

White thought of going back to Dundee, and then he thought
of the men who had been up on the girders for five hours now,
if they were still there at all. He lay off the bridge for another
hour, and put a seaman right forward, and another right aft,
with orders to hail the bridge at intervals. After each hail, a
long, drawling '*Bridge, ahoy!*', they listened. But only the wind
replied.

At last White took the *Excelsior* to Newport, but the storm
was still too bad for him to tie up there, and he went on to
Tayport, and there took a carriage to find Groethe.

'Go back to the bridge, if you please, Captain,' said the
Manager. 'Go back at low water and see if the men are safe.
Try to get them off.'

But as White took the *Excelsior* out of Tayport she ran
aground, and it was one o'clock on Saturday morning before
he was able to refloat her. The men had now been marooned
on the girders for nine hours.

Finally he got the tug back to the bridge, but still it was too
dark, floating planks still beat against the *Excelsior's* sides,
and her crew leant over with boat-hooks to fend them off.

White took her over to Dundee, and called ashore. The night-watchman shouted back that cries had been heard from the bridge. There was a thin, plaid-wrapped crowd along the Esplanade, staring into the darkness, and word came from it that cries had been heard there too.

White took the tug out again, halted her engines and listened. He heard the cries now. Thin, wordless calls like banshee notes, coming on the wind from the distant darkness. He thought also that he saw flames.

Resolutely he took the *Excelsior* right up to the piers, and even under one of the girders to the west side, and this he was able to do because water and wind had fallen slightly. He drove on to the south, to the High Girders, standing on his bridge, calling.

As quickly as it had risen ten hours before, the wind dropped and the moon came out in gentle pallor. Looking up, White now saw the hunched figures of men clinging to the piers and the girders, their rain-drenched clothes shining in the moonlight. He called.

A cry came back strongly 'We're a' fine, except McKenna and he's broken his laig!'

White brought the *Excelsior* in close to the masonry of the piers, wondering when the girders, which he knew must have fallen, would tear out the bottom of the tug. He made fast, and as his little ship heaved on the dying swell he called to the men to come down and aboard.

He counted them as they came aboard. There were thirty-nine of them, and he did not know that there had been forty when the storm struck.

On the *Excelsior*'s deck, and on the dock when they were landed, they began to talk. The sudden joy of safety loosened their tongues and they wanted to drive away their fear with talk.

John Malloch, newspaperman, was there to listen.

He heard that they had been taken out to the High Girders by the *Excelsior* at seven o'clock on Friday morning. The sky was dull, but the rain was gentle, and there seemed no reason to

cancel the day's work. The men began to work on spans 10 to
14, some on the columns, others on the girders themselves. They
worked steadily through the rain, except for two breaks of half
an hour each, when they gathered in the slat-board bothies at
the end of the girders, there to warm themselves and drink tea.

Whatever Groethe had thought of the weather as he watched
that waiting cloud, the master of the little steam launch *Tay
Bridge* had not liked it. When he had come out, in mid-after-
noon, to land more materials on the piers, he decided that the
run of the river was too ugly for him to make fast. The launch
turned with a spurt of black smoke and went back.

Towards five o'clock Foreman McKenna ordered his men to
make ready to go ashore. He expected a relief boat any moment,
and he watched for it anxiously. While he watched, the wind
and the cloud hit the southern end of the bridge, and ran
quickly along its whole length. Charles McKenna shouted to the
men on girders 12 and 13 to make their way down to the lower
spans, hold fast there and wait for the relief boat. If there were
to be relief boats, and this McKenna no longer believed.

He sat on a ram girder on top of pier 12, and with him was a
workman called John Rander. There was little shelter for any of
the men. High up, the little bothies were breaking loose, the
boards snapping off and flying into the darkness.

For four hours McKenna and Rander lay with their arms
about the iron struts, and sometimes about each other, listening to the crack and movement of iron above and below them.

Then spans 12 and 13 fell into the Tay, four hundred tons of
metal falling one hundred feet.

'For a second or two,' said McKenna, 'the air around me was
brilliantly illuminated by the friction of the falling iron.'

He lay and listened to the rush and fall of the girders, until
suddenly there was 'a feeling of excruciating pain' in his right
leg. He tried to move it and could not. He called to Rander,
whose wet hands passed gently over McKenna's body in the
darkness, and he said 'I think your leg is broken, McKenna.'

He said he would go down and get some of the men to lift
McKenna free, and down he went, seeing nothing, but feeling

with foot and hand. While he was gone the foreman managed to drag his broken leg from beneath the iron, and he crawled along the lower girders on his hands and one knee.

His friends came up slowly. There was John Wood, still desperately afraid and wondering at his escape, because he had come down from the bothies only a moment or two before the girders fell. He talked about this as he staunched the blood from McKenna's leg with a corner of his coat. McKenna, in great pain, scarcely heard him.

Rander, and another man, Henry Williamson, built a little box of planks about the foreman, and joked about it being too early for a coffin, and they covered the foreman with their own coats.

And all this was in great darkness until a tar-barrel was set afire, daubing its orange brush-strokes on the slant of the black girders. The men shouted and called until their voices were sore, and then they shouted and called again. They saw the sparks spinning from the *Excelsior*'s stack once or twice, but heard no sound from it.

Then the wind dropped and the moon came out and they looked into each other's faces and shook hands.

'I have wrought on the Tay Bridge for the last two years,' said McKenna later, and was quoted, 'but I have never experienced such a coarse night.'

At daylight on Saturday Groethe stared out to the bridge. High Girders 12 and 13 were missing. Also missing was a riveter called William Loughran, who had been out there with McKenna's crew. His absence was unnoticed until after dinner when the men lined up for their wages, and Loughran failed to answer his name. Then his friends remembered that he had spent the night on pier 10, away from the rest of them. He had been seen once only, when he crawled along until his groping hands touched a body. He asked the time. A match was struck to see, and when he was told that it was a quarter past three o'clock he crawled back, and was never seen again. It was recalled that he seemed much concerned by some inner worry.

The Reverend Mr Thomas Hill discovered what that worry might have been when he went to break the news to Mrs Loughran on Saturday afternoon. Two children tugged at her skirts as she listened to the minister, and it was quite obvious that she was about to bear the riveter a third.

On Thursday, 8 February, Albert Groethe fulfilled a previous obligation to lecture on the bridge to members of the Glasgow Athenaeum. In the course of this he gave his own opinion as to the cause of the accident.

'I will not say the girders were blown down, for that would give you the wrong idea of the matter. Though, no doubt the exceptional wind was the cause of the mishap, it could never have acted in such a manner as to blow the girders bodily off the piers. It caused the end of the girders to vibrate, and thereby shift their position in the lifting apparatus very slowly, but at last, in fact not until the gale had lasted more than three hours with unabated fury, a point was reached when the girders lost their state of equilibrium on the apparatus.

'One end fell down and broke the pins on which it had been resting from the top downward. The other end did the same for the next pin and brought the second span down also.'

The members of the Athenaeum, Mr Groethe felt sure, would be happy to learn that the value of the damage (some £3,000) would not seem so great when it was realized that it amounted to no more than one per cent of the whole cost of the undertaking.

'A work of this kind could be hardly expected to be got through from beginning to end without accident of some kind.' In fact, he said, had he delivered this lecture a week sooner he would have been able to report that there had never been an accident, quite forgetting the deaths of Herd, Stewart, Denholm, Clelland and Gellately, four years before. The chairman complimented Mr Groethe as 'a scientific and practical engineer, a most pleasing and humorous lecturer'.

And then all present were entertained by 'a dark seance, during which views of the gigantic undertaking under various aspects were exhibited by means of a magic lantern.'

# V

*'I should wish to have the opportunity
of observing the effects of high wind'*

'THE halo of incredulity,' said the newspapers, 'that only
fifteen years ago enshrouded the proposition of creating direct
railway continuity by means of a high-level bridge across the
Tay has now been dissipated, and the practicability of the pro-
ject is attested by the gigantic triumph of science by which the
Tay is spanned.'

In short, the firth was bridged.

Between Wormit and Magdalen Green, six hundred workmen,
in six years, had built a bridge with 3,700 tons of cast iron, 3,500
tons of malleable iron, 87,000 cubic feet of timber, 15,000 casks
of cement, 10,000,000 bricks, over two million rivets, and
twenty lives of men like Stewart and Denholm and Loughran.

The cost was £300,000. It had been the duty of Mr William
Paterson to see that day-by-day accounts were kept on behalf of
the North British Railway and the Tay Bridge Undertaking.
Every month the Contractors submitted their bill, and the in-
stalment was paid with promptness and courtesy. There had
been no sordid argument over money, and the successful relations in this field reflected credit on the ethical integrity of all
the gentlemen concerned. It is certain that they understood
they were not engaged in a business venture, in which all that
mattered was that one side should make a profit out of the
other, but in a mutual endeavour to increase the glory and
honour of their country. Or so much they claimed.

With a railway line now stretching across the firth from Fife
to Forfar, someone had to drive a train across it. It is true that
the line had been in use for some months, by ballast engines
carrying material out to the girders. But no real train, with car-

riages, with brake van and the ritual of a live railway company, had crossed it.

Months must yet pass before the bridge could be declared open for passenger traffic. There was, for example, the necessity of a Board of Trade inspection. The new, double line which would connect the bridge with the main line at Leuchars was already laid, and had been for some time, but there were stations yet to be finished, and time-tables to be prepared. But there was the permanent way from bank to bank, and a train could be driven across it whenever the directors of the Undertaking wished.

It was a splendid moment, and The Great McGonagall, 'poet and tragedian' of Dundee, and master of bathetic verse, responded to its inspiration.

> Beautiful Railway Bridge of the Silvery Tay!
> I hope that God will protect all passengers
> By night and by day,
> And that no accident will befall them while crossing
> The Bridge of the Silvery Tay,
> For that would be most awful to be seen
> Near by Dundee and the Magdalen Green.

Lesser poets caught at the rainbow simile and repeated it, ignoring or forgetting that old Patrick Matthew had seen this too, and dreaded it. A rainbow was a beautiful thing, the Almighty's bridge across the sky. The Tay Bridge was a beautiful thing too, and the crock of gold at its foot was far more tangible.

The directors of the North British and of the Undertaking decided to make the first crossing (and who else should make it?) on 26 September 1877.

It was a handsome day, with a golden sun bringing out the reds and yellows and russet browns of the Fifeshire hills. Some of the gentlemen assembled at Leuchars station early in the forenoon, formal, self congratulatory in new broadcloth, biblical beards, and shining top hats. They awaited the special from Burntisland, bringing other gentlemen, and when it came,

somewhat late it must be admitted, it was the tiny engine
'Lochee', with green body and glistening brass almost hidden by
bunting, the Union flag and the lion of Scotland. It drew behind
it a saloon and a first class coach, and two brake vans. In the
saloon were baskets of wine and cold collation should the
gentlemen or the ladies be unable to wait for lunch.

From Burntisland came old Kippen Davie, of course, a great
man at this moment, and for whom the Ordinary shareholders
of the North British must be thanking God devoutly. There was
his deputy chairman Mr John Beaumont. There was Sir James
Falshaw, without whose presence no Tay Bridge junket appears
to have been complete. There was a handful of Scottish
Members of Parliament. There were other gentlemen of Glasgow and Edinburgh and Stirling and Perth, and there was a band
to play lilting Scottish airs, reels, strathspeys and marches.

The gentlemen from Burntisland got out at Leuchars to
stretch their legs and to greet James Cox and Mr Yeaman, and to
congratulate each other on the fine weather, remarking that it
must surely be taken as a good omen. Then all got back aboard.

On the footplate of the little 'Lochee' was no ordinary engine-
driver. He was the great Dugald Drummond, locomotive superintendent for the North British Railway, a craggy, explosive
man who would have torn any other man from the engine on
this occasion. Drummond was a great figure in Scottish railway
history, 'a rough mon but awfu' just', and the memory of him
lives in a hundred railway histories that genuflect with rever-
ence and humour before the engines he built.

A blaspheming, profaning, pious, angry, kindly man by turns,
a hard-rock foundation on which stood the sometimes crazy
superstructure of his company, it was only right that he should
be the first to drive a train along the greatest bridge in the
world. So he drove it. His beard jutted beyond the little locomotive's side, and if he swore at this or that, as he usually did,
no doubt his anger was directed at his superiors that day and
not his workmen.

In twenty minutes the special had reached the south abutment of the bridge, and there Dugald Drummond brought his

train to a halt and leaned out of the cab, and said little or nothing to Bouch's inspector, Henry Noble, a painstaking man but with little ability. Probably Drummond thought that a bridge was a bridge, and any fool could design one, but only a man with a soul could create a lovely, living thing like a railway engine.

The train had stopped to take aboard more passengers, including Mrs Margaret Bouch, Mrs Gilkes, and a General Delpratt of Amsterdam (who had paid the bridge a visit some years before and stayed on to help his countryman Camphuis in its construction). During the halt Minister Thomson of Forgan prayed heartily and long, while the ladies bowed their heads and the gentlemen held their hats close to the left breast.

A pilot engine set off across the bridge, whistling cheerfully, with Thomas Bouch on the footplate. The special followed.

Along the high land at Wormit the crowd cheered and waved handkerchiefs and parasols in the sun, and there was a flutter of handkerchiefs from the carriage windows as the train left the high ground, moving on to the first spans, where the clacking of its wheels changed to a deeper, more sonorous rumble.

The crossing took fifteen minutes. To the west of the bridge the steamers *Star o' Gowrie*, *Star o' Tay*, and *Excelsior*, a cloud of yachts, fishing-boats, and wherries, crowded with colour, filled the river. On the far shore, along Magdalen Green and the Esplanade, many thousands of people watched a train on a bridge, a lonely, unreal thing crawling along a great thread.

When the train entered the High Girders, and was suddenly enclosed on all sides by the fret and lattice of iron that spun by the windows with quick-slanting shadows, the noise of the wheels changed to a roar, and some of the ladies paled, and looked across to their husbands who were smiling and nodding reassuringly.

Half-way through the Girders there was the sudden smack of wood, the noise of splintering, and a *lackety-lackety-lack* beating on the roofs of the carriages, and then a mirthless wrench of metal as the ventilation cowlings were carried away. The ladies screamed.

A gentleman put his head out of the window, staring back, with the air-stream blowing his hair about his red face, and when he pulled himself inside he explained that some idiot of a workman had left wooden staging in the path of the train, and this had been struck. That was all. Now the ladies smiled, but it had been a thrilling moment.

The train turned as it neared the north bank, clattered over the bow-string girders and dropped down to the new marshalling yards, and at last came to a stop. Two thousand people were crowded up against the walls of the yards, and small boys were dancing and yelling and waving their caps. The gentlemen made a quick tour of the yards, making it as brief as possible, for the ladies were asking about lunch.

After lunch the ladies and gentlemen returned to the special and were 'whirled' across the bridge at 25 miles an hour back to Edinburgh. The bridge had been built, the bridge had been crossed by train.

Oh, beautiful railway bridge, wrote the Great McGonagall.

> Beautiful Railway Bridge of the Silvery Tay!
> And prosperity to Provost Cox, who has given
> Thirty thousand pounds and upwards away
> In helping to erect the Bridge of the Tay,
> Most handsome to be seen,
> Near by Dundee and the Magdalen Green.

The winter passed and the directors of the Undertaking decided that the bridge was now ready to receive its inspection by the Board of Trade. So up to Dundee, in the month of February, came Major-General Charles Scrope Hutchinson, Royal Engineers, Board of Trade Inspector, a stiff, scrupulous, exacting man, who had a sharp eye for the inconsequential detail. Once, when investigating the cause of an accident, in which the boiler of a locomotive had burst and killed its driver, the Major-General discovered and gravely noted in his report that travelling on the footplate at the time, as an unauthorized passenger, had been a wine and spirits merchant. He drew no conclusions from this, but appeared to think it important.

He spent three days examining the bridge from end to end, and another two weeks considering his report before he wrote it. He was much occupied during those three days, and he was accompanied by Thomas Bouch, anxious and willing to give every assistance.

The tests were very thorough, up to one point, and to test that point the Major-General would have required some assistance from the weather, which he did not get. To test for vertical dead weight he used ballast engines, first one travelling across the girders alone, and then two coupled together, then three, four, five and finally six. He ran them across at various speeds, the fastest being 40 miles an hour, and while they were doing this he had himself hauled up inside one of the iron piers under the High Girders, with his note-book, and his hat clamped firmly on his head.

Then he had it all done again while he stood at Wormit with a theodolite, directing it on the top of the High Girders to observe lateral oscillation. He went out in a little steam launch and watched the trains thundering across again. The oscillation, he said later, was 'nothing at all excessive, as far as my judgement went'.

Mr Gilkes had suggested that the ballast engines travel across at 40 miles an hour, and to this the Major-General agreed, timing them with his stop-watch. He discovered that they went through the thousand-odd yards of the High Girders in 52 seconds.

But he paid no great attention to wind pressure. Two years later, when he was asked why, he said 'The subject of wind pressure never entered into the calculations that I made, and never have done . . . We have had no data whatever to go upon with regard to wind pressure. It has never been, to my knowledge, customary hitherto to take wind pressure into account in calculating the parts of bridges of this description.'

His report gave a general description of the bridge, and was careful to point out that its designer was 'T. Bouch, Esq., M.I.C.E.' He made only the most trivial suggestions for improvement.

He suggested that transoms and ties for preserving the gauge should be provided between the longitudinals. He thought that the fireproof covering of the floor was badly in need of repair, here and there. Some slack places in the rails, he thought, required adjusting, and 'to reduce as much as possible the expansions of the girders in hot weather I should strongly recommend their being painted white'.

It was not desirable, he said, that trains should travel over the bridge at high speeds. 'I would suggest 25 miles an hour as a limit that should not be exceeded.'

He made one final observation, almost at the end of the report, before he signed himself 'I have &c, C. S. Hutchinson, R.E.' This qualification did much, two years later, to save him from the blame, the anger, and the mob-hatred suffered by Thomas Bouch.

'When again visiting the spot,' wrote the General, 'I should wish, if possible, to have an opportunity of observing the effects of a high wind when a train of carriages is running over the bridge.'

It was his only reference to the possible effect of wind pressure. But he never made the visit. He meant to, of course, but he fell ill, and another officer was assigned the final duty of inspecting the railways north and south of the bridge, and this officer had neither the time nor the inclination to wait for a high wind and a railway train.

The last formality was over. In the spring of 1878 the Tay bridge glittered across the estuary in bright varnish; its total length from signal cabin to signal cabin was 1 mile, 1,705 yards.

It rested on 85 piers, the first fourteen of which, stepping out from the south bank, were of brick, the rest of them iron columns which, in the spring sunlight, threw chequered patterns of shadow on the silver water. So fascinating were these shadows that boatmen were hired to take parties of ladies and gentlemen out into the river to see them, and to listen to the wind sighing a lament through the iron.

It was not a straight bridge, not an arm thrust directly from bank to bank and joining each to the other with tense iron sinews. From the south shore it curved left for three spans, bringing itself at right angles to the course of the river which, at that point, ran due west to east. Then it turned to the right again, as if uncertain how to make the terrible crossing.

For the first three spans, too, it fell slightly in height, then running level for another three, and climbing again, like a tired wave, in an incline of 1 in 490, to Pier 29. There it ran level once more until, at Pier 36, it began to fall. The incline from Pier 36 to 37 was 1 in 130, after which the fall was rapid, about 1 in 74, until the north shore was reached. It swung to the right in a wide curve as it reached the Forfar bank. Up and down, wavering as its iron and concrete legs sought firm foundation, it was a giant centipede treading the water.

Its highest portion, of course, was where the High Girders lifted their skirts in deference to Perth's surly demand for free shipway. Bouch had won a partial victory, aided by Stirling. The High Girders were not 100 feet from high water, but 88. Yet it was 169 feet from the top of the girders to the river-bed, and the foundations went 20 feet or more below that.

Here were thirteen great spans, eleven of 245 feet and two of 227 feet. They made a tunnel of open ironwork, and workmen had already discovered that when the ballast engines passed through it they set up strange gyrations in the air, and a mournful humming as the currents fought to escape upward and outward through the latticed struts. It was a tunnel 27 feet high and 14 feet across, and it was a wonderful thing. Whoever first called it The High Girders, capitalizing the words to emphasize them, had touched the whole structure with poetry.

The piers that supported the central spans stood on iron and concrete caissons that reached just above high water mark, 31 feet in diameter, lined with 18 inches of brickwork. They were sunk deep in the gravel, resting on rock where possible, or on Gerrit Camphuis' piles.

Each iron pier above the base consisted of six iron columns, bolted together vertically by means of cross-bracing and struts of wrought iron. These were held to the masonry base on a hexagonal floor, at the angles of which were six cast-iron base-pieces, 2 feet high, and secured to the pier by 1¾ inch bolts that passed down through two 15-inch stone courses.

Until the novelty palled, people would row out to the piers to stare at and finger this puzzle of iron and stone. And since they were not iron-founders or engineers, but shop-keepers and clerks and factory-workers, they could not say whether the workmanship was good or bad, whether the iron was adequately cast and the black varnish did not hide treacherous blown-holes. They did not know whether the bolts on the piers were held snug or tight, or whether the tide-water was already seeping in and rusting and rotting them.

So there the bridge was at last, and Fife was a railway island no longer. The way lay open south to Burntisland and the Firth of Forth, and Mr Bouch was already working on his bridge to cross that too.

There was the bridge at last, stepping through 45 feet of water and a tidal run of 5 knots. For weeks the Press, the lecture halls, the magic lanterns 'in dark seance,' fed the people of Dundee with the wonders of the new bridge, until even schoolboys could tell each other that it would take a rolling load of 1½ tons to the foot run, although this load could not be reached even though each span were filled with loaded wagons. Further, the iron spans would also take a strain of 21 tons to the square inch, but since the most it would ever be asked to take was four, the idea that it might collapse was laughable.

One correspondent, writing at length on his profound admiration for the bridge, said that he had been told by the contractors (and presumably this was Albert Groethe talking) that 'as the open lattice work of the girders offers but little resistance to the wind, there is no tendency of these swaying sideways'.

It seemed reasonable. In fact there appeared to be nothing at all that could tear this slender ribbon from its hold on land, water and sky.

The permanent way that mounted the bridge consisted of double-headed steel rails, fished at the joints, in 24 feet lengths, weighing 75 lb. to the yard, and held by oak keys in cast-iron chairs. There was an oak flooring of three-inch planks, painted with a water-proof covering that not only prevented rotting by water but burning by fallen embers.

Carried across the river by the bridge was the main water pipe from Dundee to Newport. A guard-rail, which was also a gas pipe, gave hand-hold for the workmen who were to maintain the bridge. Also carried were thirteen telegraph cables held in an iron tube and boxed in wood. It had been found wiser to pass such cables along the length of the bridge, rather than sinking them to the river-bed where ship's anchors fouled and broke them.

There was much praise for the cement foundations, this Portland cement, fine, greyish-green powder which, when set, as it did set in a day or so, was as hard and as firm as stone. 'Without it,' wrote Albert Groethe (in *Good Words*, of course), 'the building of the Tay Bridge would in all probability have been impossible.'

When all superlatives in praise of the bridge had been exhausted, attention was turned to the sidings and goods yards at Wormit, built on land so reluctantly relinquished by the Laird of Birkhill. They ran back 600 yards from the beginning of the bridge, and were 80 yards broad. There wagons of coal, minerals, food were to await their turn to cross the bridge to Dundee.

Further south, along the new line to Leuchars, new stations had been built, the most impressive being at a junction north of Leuchars, a handsome, efficient building with a suite of waiting-rooms, the licence for which had been smartly secured by Mr Orchison of Arbroath, who was now ready to delight the passengers as soon as the North British could bring them along to him. Further north, as the new railway looped through a cutting to break upon the bridge, was the last station of the line – St Fort. Its agent was to be Robert Morris, a man meticulous in his habits and duties, as was to be later proved.

But the new works in Fifeshire were nothing compared with the transformation that had taken place across the Tay at Dundee. There the foreshore had been built up into a handsome esplanade, a viaduct of 1,000 feet, a wall of 4,000 feet, and 5 feet thick. Behind these the new goods shed, the marshalling yards that branched like the veins of a chestnut leaf from the single stem that came across the Tay.

In the city was the new Tay Bridge Station, the North British Railway's firm and irremovable foot across the river. It was a low-level station with a central platform, 380 feet long, beneath a glass roof that was a matter of great pride, but which was to cause the station-master great worry later. To the east of the station was the new tunnel which, skirting the Harbour, took the line on to Arbroath and Aberdeen.

It was worth the price of a platform ticket to go down and admire the waiting-room plumbing of Mr Mackie, or Mr McRitchie's plasterwork, Mr Buttar's slates, and Mr Keay's tasteful ironwork. It was a pity that a painter could not have been found in Dundee also, but it was admitted that Mr Forsyth of Edinburgh had done extremely well. The station was built of soft-hued grey stone from Bannockburn, giving 'a remarkably clean and finished appearance'.

The Press was gratified to learn that facilities included 'extensive lavatory accommodation, porter's room, hot-water room, lamp-room, three classes of ladies' waiting-rooms, gentlemen's waiting-rooms, three refreshment rooms of different classes, left luggage-room, luggage and parcel lifts, station-master's room, and ticket offices'.

The upper floors, fronting on South Union Street and looking across to the harbour, contained a magnificent dining-room, 70 feet in length, glittering with metal and glass, and the dull glow of polished wood. Altogether it was a fine and fitting station to await the arrival of trains crossing the finest and longest and the greatest bridge in the world. A Scottish bridge, even though it had been designed by an Englishman.

Beautiful, wrote the Great McGonagall,

> Beautiful Railway Bridge of the Silvery Tay!
> Which will cause great rejoicing on the opening day,
> And hundreds of people will come from far away,
> Also the Queen, most gorgeous to be seen,
> Near by Dundee and the Magdalen Green.

# VI

*'Blondin crossing Niagara'*

BUT the Queen did not come. Late in May 1878 word arrived
from Balmoral. Sir Henry Ponsonby expressed Her Majesty's regret that it would not be possible for her to attend The Grand
Opening of The Tay Bridge. Nobody had really believed that the
old lady would come. Without the presence of dear Albert, dead
these seventeen years, such public occasions could still be a
bitter experience. Like everyone else, the civic leaders of
Dundee were somewhat bored by this prolonged bereavement,
and hoped that she might break it by sharing their pride. They
had to content themselves with her good wishes, which were
graciously, if somewhat remotely, expressed.

The inauguration of a passenger train service across the Firth
of Tay was set for Friday, 31 May 1878. The North British Railway, the Tay Bridge Undertaking, the City Council of Dundee,
Mr Phin the grocer, Mr Leng the newspaper owner, everybody
was determined to make it a memorable day. Even the weather,
with its usual two-faced malevolence, decided to offer this day
the mask which smiled. For once a wind blew from the south-
east, soft and warm. The sun broke in sharp squares and rec-
tangles on the multi-green fields along the Carse of Gowrie. The
air was so clean that from the south bank could be seen the
clear outlines of the farm houses and towns below the Sidlaws.
There were smudges of white steam and black smoke from the
jute factories, of course, but these seemed only the more colour-
ful against the blue sky.

Most remarkable was the manner in which the sun shone on
the fashionable stained-glass that filled the windows of the villas
in Newport.

Two special parties were to have the honour of making the

inauguration journey. The first came from Dundee, the second from Edinburgh. They were to meet and join the train at Leuchars.

The Dundee party boarded the steamer *Auld Reekie* early in the morning, and the gentlemen 'lounged about the boat in apparent appreciation of the delightful sail'. The ladies sat in the stern under their parasols, with the brilliant folds of their skirts flowing over the white deck. They were welcomed ashore at Tayport by the Camperdown Linen Works Band which, all in red and blue and gold, and under its conductor Mr Andrew Johnston, blew its brassy way through several national airs, both Highland and Lowland. From all the windows of Newport flew either the Union flag or the lion of Scotland. Amid a flutter of handkerchiefs the party boarded a train for Leuchars.

The Edinburgh party left Waverley Station at 9.35 a.m. Taking the train to Granton, it there boarded the steamer *John Stirling*, telling itself that it would not be many years before Mr Bouch had bridged the Forth too. In fact, if one looked away towards Inchgarvie one could see a solid block of concrete, 31 feet square and 13 high, which might be the first pier of the new bridge. One was living at a dramatic moment of history.

At Burntisland the train that was to travel north across the Tay to Dundee was waiting with steam up. Nearly 300 people boarded it, and set off in the shining claret carriages, behind the puffing green and brass engine.

At Leuchars there was a wait of twenty minutes for the Dundee party, no great hardship, after all, for 'the Refreshment Room was well-patronized, and the refreshments were of a sort that reflected credit on the purveyor who was assiduous to those who called upon his services'.

Finally the 'Lochee' steamed out of Leuchars, pulling 'a numerous array of first-class carriages containing 1,500 ladies and gentlemen'. A happy train, full of laughter and gentle talk, of pompous eulogies and wild ambition, moving along the lovely vale of Motray Water below St Michael's Wood, where the country-folk had lined the cuttings to wave their bonnets. It rattled through St Fort, where Station Agent Morris, in gold banded top hat and frock-coat, had assembled his little staff. Here the 'Lochee' dropped speed a little, so that the passengers might admire the smartness and efficiency of even the smallest station on the great North British line.

Within five minutes the train was then taking the northern bend past Wormit Farm, bringing it to the bridge. There was 'a general rising in the seats' as the passengers crowded to the windows on the left to get their first glimpse of the bridge, shining black in the sun. Then, as the train turned again, they moved to the other windows to see a river thick with boats, a great splash of broken colour on the silver water. On these vessels the waiting crowds had seen the 'Lochee's' white plume jutting from the cutting, and they began to cheer. The cheering continued and grew louder as the engine rumbled on to the bridge past Thomas Barclay's signal cabin. It was his first train across, and he stood to attention on the boarding below his hut.

It was a smooth, uneventful crossing at the 25 miles an hour stipulated by General Hutchinson. Until the train reached the High Girders there was nothing to prove to the passengers that they were on a bridge at all. They seemed to be travelling gently through the air, eighty feet above the water. But once they reached the High Girders the iron swept up and embraced them, and for most of them this was a reassuring sight. There was, however, some slight vibration now, exaggerated by the excitement, and giving palpitations to a few of the ladies.

Below, on a steamer in the river, the Special Correspondent from *The Times* looked up at the little train pushing its way so slowly across the bridge. He had a felicitous thought, and made a note of it immediately lest the events of the day should drive it from his mind. Seeing it all, he thought, 'excited the same kind of nervousness as must have been felt by those watching Blondin crossing Niagara'.

By 12.37 p.m. the special was over the bridge, travelling more rapidly now, down the incline, through the bowstring, round the curve, to a flutter of hats and bonnets and handkerchiefs along the Esplanade. The grass of Magdalen Green was almost hidden by thousands of men and women all waving.

The 'Lochee' drew up on the north platform of Tay Bridge Station, and as it released one last great expiring sigh of steam, Provost Robertson was ready waiting to greet John Stirling, the first to alight.

Stirling had scarcely two feet on the platform before Robertson was reaching for his hand and shouting, with great emotion, 'I bid you a right hearty welcome! I am delighted to welcome you!'

There were cheers and handclaps that stopped when the Provost held up his hand, and the town officers beat the hafts of their Lochaber axes on the platform.

Stirling said 'I believe the bridge will do more to promote the prosperity of Dundee than anything that has occurred for many years.' Which was just what everybody wanted to hear.

More handclaps, with the ladies coming from the carriages now, with skirts uplifted away from the dust, the gentlemen baring their heads and smiling. James Cox, as chairman of the Tay Bridge Undertaking, announced that it fell to him to declare the bridge open and ready for traffic, 'to be wrought hereafter by the North British Railway Company'.

'The Tay Bridge,' he said, 'is a structure worthy of this enlightened age!' Which, once again, was what everyone wished to hear.

Then the ladies and gentlemen who had invitations for the great banquet in the Albert Hall, formed themselves into a procession and walked up the steps of South Union Street behind a detachment of police, behind the town officers with their axes, behind good John Stirling smiling shortsightedly. Once he came into view from the street the band of the First Forfarshire Volunteers broke into 'See the Conquering Hero Comes!' All the steamers in the river whooped and brayed, the bells in Old Steeple rang, the ladies put their hands over their ears against the noise.

Off went the Forfarshires, with the procession forming behind. Up South Union Street. To the right along Nethergate into the High Street. Up Reform Street to Meadowside and the Albert Hall, with flags flickering along the kerbs, and neatly

aligned rows of schoolchildren cheering at their teachers' signal
and sucking sticks of Tay Bridge Rock.

In Albert Square the Forfarshires took their instruments from
their mouths, lifted their shakoes and wiped their faces. The
gentlemen fell into easy disorder to climb past flanking ever-
greens into the hall, each holding an invitation card which,
measuring eight inches by five inches, had been too large to go
into their pockets and had been held in their hands since they
left home that morning.

The members of the Joint Committee of the Tay Bridge Undertaking, and the Chairman and Directors of the North British Railway, request the favour of your company on the occasion of the
opening of the Tay Bridge and Railways at Dundee on the 31st current.

Before lunch, which was to be a 'substantial dinner' spiced
with the new Tay Bridge Sauce invented for the occasion by a
pharmaceutical chemist of the city, there was one important
ceremony. At a hasty meeting that morning the Town Council
had decided to give the Freedom of the Burgh to both Bouch
and Stirling.

Stirling was present to receive it, of course, but Thomas
Bouch was not. His sensitive nature could not endure the
speeches, the bands playing 'Conquering Hero', the cheers, the
waving of flags. He sent his regrets. There was, after all, the
Forth Bridge to be designed. He was sure the gentlemen would
understand.

So the Provost asked Mr Stirling if he would get word to Mr
Bouch somehow, and arrange a convenient meeting in the
Town Hall at which Mr Bouch might be properly and officially
vested with the Freedom of the Ancient Burgh of Dundee.
There was a murmur of approval only marred by Mr Wieland,
who said that if Mr Bouch had had any idea of the honour that
was to be paid him he would undoubtedly have been present. If
anyone took this, as Mr Wieland intended they should take it, as
a sharp inference that the civic leaders should have made up
their minds earlier, it was discreetly ignored.

So everybody went in to lunch, 'a very elegant one purveyed by Mr Russell and well served by a staff of waiters from Edinburgh and Glasgow'. When it was over there was the moving of toasts, which were proposed in order of precedence. To:

The Queen, the Prince and Princess of Wales and other members of the Royal Family.
The Army, Navy, and Reserve Forces.
The Two Houses of Parliament.
The Tay Bridge Undertaking.
The Provost, Magistrates and Town Council of Dundee.
The Scottish Burghs.
The Engineer of the Tay Bridge Undertaking.
The Railways of the United Kingdom.
The Lord Lieutenants and Sheriffs of Fife and Forfar.
The Directors of the North British Railway.
The Manufacturing and Mercantile Interest.
The Contractors for the Tay Bridge Railway.

When Stirling spoke his words were gentle and modest, but he allowed himself the boast that he had never been one to disparage the idea of the bridge, but had had faith in it from the beginning, at which there was great applause from the gentlemen, most of whom had only recently ceased to regard Bouch as a maniac and his bridge as a dream.

Replying to the toast to the armed services Admiral Maitland Dougall, ret., referred briefly to the bridge and hurried on to speak of Britain's splendid Navy, at that very moment serving the country all over the world. If there were to be a war with Russia he knew that the lads would show themselves worthy of their great traditions. He was followed by Colonel Walker, who said that while he was not a great critic of bridges or wars (laughter) he would say that the Volunteer Forces had never been seen in so great a state of efficiency. Admiral Dougall had spoken of war with Russia. He would not dwell on this, but would remind all present of the high degree of training, devotion, and courage to be found among the soldiers of the Queen, both regular and volunteer. This, too, Russia might well consider.

Following Members of Parliament took up this theme with vigour and wider vocabulary, and the Chairman had to bring the attention of the room back to the bridge as he proposed The Tay Bridge Undertaking, in which he could 'not but pay a passing tribute to Mr Bouch'.

Outside the Albert Hall Mr Warren and the First Forfarshire were still playing. A crowd of 15,000 was waiting, perhaps because, having given the day over to this celebration, they had nothing better to do, or perhaps because some of them were hoping that the emergence of the lunchers would (judging by the time spent inside) be less dignified and more entertaining than their entry.

At last it was all over, and the carriages clopped up to the steps of the Albert Hall and took the lunchers away. The evening papers were already on the streets, roundly declaring that this matter of Mr Bouch's Freedom should have been decided much earlier, 'but it is never too late to do a graceful thing'.

The Forfarshires marched away down Reform Street playing lively airs, with urchins skipping about and behind them. From somewhere or other appeared the Camperdown Linen Works Band under Mr Johnston, to march just as musically in the opposite direction. The children who had lined the streets licked the last of their Tay Bridge Rock from their fingers and went home. There was nothing to do now but run a railway.

The company had issued its first time-table the evening before, announcing that it would run seven trains a day from Dundee to Edinburgh, and seven from Edinburgh to Dundee, and that Mr James Smith, station-master at Polmont Junction, had been appointed to the new Tay Bridge Station.

Basically no different from the old, the new time-table made encouraging reading by virtue of the fact that it cut the journey to Edinburgh by an hour. The first train of the day was to leave Dundee at 6.25 a.m., stopping at all stations through Fife and arriving at Burntisland on the Forth at 8.18. But it was not the train to catch if one were going to Edinburgh, for the Forth ferryboat would not leave Burntisland before the arrival of the 7.15 from Dundee. This would come in at 8.30 a.m.

The ferry would then sail, and passengers would arrive in

Edinburgh at 9.35 a.m., after a journey of two hours and twenty minutes.

The regular passenger service began on Saturday, June the first, and for the whole of that day people travelled to and fro like children with a new plaything. Most of them took tickets to St Fort or Leuchars and picnicked in the hills before returning. They left as early as they could. The 6.25 a.m. pulled out of Tay Bridge Station with 850 men, women and children aboard, anxious to be the first ordinary passengers to cross the Firth of Tay by railway bridge.

They were not. At five a.m. a goods train had come over from Fife, carrying 30 black-faced wedders for slaughter by a butcher of Dundee.

The journey was not to everybody's satisfaction. The *Dundee Advertiser* pointed out that most of the trains were either late in arriving, or late in leaving, but it added charitably that it supposed some allowance should be made on the first day. The public, less charitable, loudly complained to the booking-clerks that the fares were excessive. It had believed that the journey to St Fort would cost no more than sixpence, why had the North British fixed the rate at ninepence?

'Unless the Company makes some concessions,' said the *Advertiser* on Monday morning, 'they will not popularize the Tay Bridge locally.'

# ENTR'ACTE

*'With sea-mews wheeling beneath us'*

AT night, people who lived along the Tayside would turn down the gaslight, the better to watch the trains crossing the Tay Bridge.

It was hard to determine which was the more wondrous. A dark, moonless night when the bridge could not be seen, and the lights of the train appeared from nowhere at Wormit and glided by a graceful miracle through the sky to Magdalen Green. Or a night when the moon was full, and the fine lacework of the girders was clearly visible, the faery wonder of Mr Bouch's greatest achievement.

On summer evenings, particularly those when there were very low tides and it was sometimes possible to walk out into the river to My Lord's Bank, there was bathing below the Esplanade in the long, sharp shadows of the girders. Children pulled rich green strands of seaweed from the masonry, and lovers cut their initials on the concrete.

Visitors to Dundee, commercial travellers who had once been forced to endure the agony of the double ferry crossing of the firths, now wrote to the Dundee newspapers expressing their delight at being able to cross the Tay in such comfort 'with the sea-mews wheeling beneath us'.

Land values on south Tayside rose rapidly. A railway was built, connecting the bridge with Newport and thus turning the little town into a dormitory suburb. New villas were built there for Dundee businessmen, all with glittering, stained-glass windows.

The new line had been expensive, but it would, as The Great McGonagall pointed out,

> ... clear all expenses in a very short time;
> Because the thrifty housewives of Newport
> To Dundee will often resort,
> Which will be to them profit and sport,
> By bringing cheap tea, bread and jam,
> And also some of Lipton's ham.

The Laird of Birkhill, who had once fought to keep the North British from obtaining one inch of his land, now announced himself only too happy to accommodate the railway in any way possible. 'With enlightened appreciation of his own interests as a landed proprietor' he asked the North British to build a station at Wormit on the Newport branch line. The Company agreed to pay for such a station as soon as the Laird had erected twenty-five houses on the spot. Mr Wedderburn happily consented, and sold the land-plots at a good profit.

There was no cause for despondency. From his offices at 4 Princes Street Edinburgh, James Cox, chairman of the Undertaking, issued a statement to shareholders. If they wished, he said, they might now dispose of their stock at the rate of £130 for each £100 of shares. He had £30,000 in the Undertaking, and was leaving it there.

To the North British Railway the bridge brought a prosperity beyond the most sanguine hopes of its directors. Within a year of its opening, John Walker, General Manager, estimated that the Company was now carrying 84 per cent of the Dundee–Edinburgh traffic, and 59 per cent of the Edinburgh–Aberdeen traffic. Traffic between Dundee and Fifeshire had been doubled, season tickets had increased by 100 per cent. The Fife coal-fields had been opened up to a degree impossible while the ferry-system was still in operation. In six months the goods and mineral traffic to Dundee rose by 40 per cent.

The North British now dominated the railway industry in the north of Scotland. It had over 500 locomotives, over 1,000 carriages and nearly 30,000 wagons. It was carrying over 15,000,000 passengers, and taking a total revenue of more than £2,000,000 a year.

One thing only was needed to make the directors of the

Undertaking completely happy – the favour of the Queen. In the late June of 1879 it was known that she was at Balmoral and would shortly be returning to Windsor. Why should she not make this journey across the bridge, instead of by way of Perth?

Before this question could be put to Her Majesty's advisers it was answered for them. One Monday an engine came down the line from the north, pulling the empty double-saloon coach which had been specially built for the Queen, and which was normally kept at Ballater. With all the signals deferring to it, it ran smartly through Tay Bridge Station, up the incline and on to the bridge. It crossed to the south bank, stopped, and ran back. Satisfied that the bridge would not collapse beneath it, the Royal coach went back to Ballater.

Delighted by this somewhat blunt indication of Her Majesty's intentions, Baillie Thomson, Baillie Low, and Baillie Maxwell, representing the Town Council, set off sharply for Balmoral in their Sabbath best. They took with them the humble plea that 'it was the desire of the community that the Queen should, on the occasion of passing through Dundee, make a short stay during which time she might visit the Albert Institute, erected to the memory of the Prince Consort, and receive from the Corporation an address of welcome.'

The three men were received by Sir Henry Ponsonby, who listened to them politely and said that of course Her Majesty proposed to return to England by way of the new bridge, but all arrangements had been made and it was impossible for them to be altered to the extent of breaking her journey.

Having discovered that their subtle appeal to the Royal widow's grief had not succeeded, Baillie Thomson tried a second attack. He produced a vellum-bound album of pictures (more handsome than that given to General Grant, of course) and handed it to Sir Henry. He explained that while it contained some views and plans of the bridge it also contained some very fine pictures of the Albert Institute which might please Her Majesty when she could find the time, among her duties, to study them.

Sir Henry thanked the baillies, entertained them with refreshments, and saw them to their carriage. They went back to Dundee with the feeling that the citizens of that burgh were going to be thoroughly dissatisfied. It was now Wednesday, and the Queen would be travelling down at the week-end.

But the next day there arrived for Baillie Thomson a post-haste letter from Sir Henry. Probably the tasteful pictures of the Albert Institute had touched the Queen, and she desired Sir Henry to inform the Corporation that she would be most happy to have her train halted at Tay Bridge station and receive the Corporation address through the window of her coach.

But no address had yet been written, so a meeting of magistrates was hurriedly called to compose it.

The Royal train left Ballater in bright sunshine on Friday afternoon. Crowds lined the cuttings and embankments all the way, calling 'God Bless Your Majesty!' to the black-clothed, dumpy figure half-hidden by the window-curtains. On Tay Bridge Station a black, gold, scarlet and tartan cloud of Councillors, Lord Lieutenants, Members of Parliament, Volunteer Officers, bandsmen, jute manufacturers, flax spinners, policemen, and railway employees, were waiting and listening anxiously to the telegraph reports of Her Majesty's journey down the line.

She was at Aberdeen. She was at Bridge of Dun. She was at Arbroath (and two minutes late, but not, thank God, due to the inefficiency of the North British Railway). She was at Carnoustie and it was 5.39. She would be at Dundee within twenty minutes.

The bells of Old Steeple had begun to ring at 5 p.m. There was bunting on all ships in the harbour. On board the *Mars*, three-quarters of a mile from the bridge, the boys were on deck in their best uniforms, ready to man the yards. There were flags hanging from the windows in Reform Street, and a great crowd waited outside the Albert Institute which, it was confidently believed, the old widow would be sure to visit, no matter what Sir Henry and Baillie Thomson might have said.

Lost in the great crowd on the platform was a bearded, silent

man, his face locked fast in an iron expression of impassivity.
Thomas Bouch was there with his wife and his son.

Messrs Mackie and Howe had put a handsome red carpet
along the greater part of the platform that morning, and kept a
man there all afternoon to brush it every time an incautious
foot marked it. John Stewart, horticulturist of Dundee, had
placed some of his prize stove plants close to the stanchions,
and these were much admired. Flanked by halberd men,
weighted by the chain of his office, Provost Brownlee stood in
the centre of the platform, clasping the address of welcome
which the magistrates had finished composing only twenty
hours before, and on which Mr David Maclaren, architect to the
Dundee School Board, had spent the night hours, copying it on
vellum in old English script. A great seal hung from it by a
scarlet ribbon.

At 5.54 the Royal train was signalled at Camperdown Station,
and three minutes later it burst out of the Dock Street tunnel in
an explosion of steam, and halted at Tay Bridge Station.

When the steam died away there was the old lady in her poke
bonnet behind the lowered window, smiling gently at the ladies
and gentlemen and the officers and the stove plants. As the last
clash of the National Anthem died away the Provost stepped
forward, read the address in good Scots, and presented it to Her
Majesty, who smiled and handed it to her Lady in Waiting.

Up at the front of the platform the North British engine
'Netherby' was being coupled to the train, with James Mclaren,
General Superintendent of the line, on the foot-plate.

The Queen was presented to Thomas Bouch who bowed
stiffly, to John Stirling, to James Cox, and then, over their shoulders, she saw a familiar face – Sir John Richardson of Pitfour.
She beckoned him to her. Was it not sad, she asked as he leant
forward to catch her whispered words, to hear of the unfortunate death of the Prince Imperial in Zululand?

With that, the seven minutes' halt was over. The 'Netherby'
gave a discreet whistle. Her Majesty waved, sat back, and the
train moved off.

As it climbed the incline toward the bridge it passed through the ranks of a hundred and forty boys from the *Mars*, some of them at the salute with muskets, a score more playing the National Anthem under the direction of a tartan-trewed Corporal of the 72nd Highlanders. Along the Esplanade ladies and gentlemen stood up in their carriages to look over the wall and wave their handkerchiefs. Her Majesty waved hers briefly.

At eight minutes past six the train turned on to the bridge. James Mclaren brought its speed well down, and the train took twice the normal time to cross the bridge. The tide was running at half-full, the sun was striking the water at an acute angle from the west, turning its urbane face copper. There was a gilded haze over the Carse of Gowrie. The guns of the *Mars*, one by one, spat out little fluffs of cotton wool. And below the High Girders, as the train went by, six long-boats, full of more boys from the *Mars*, tossed oars in salute.

Wormit signal box, Thomas Barclay at attention, was passed at 6.21 p.m. Her Majesty was last seen looking gravely down the river to the sea.

It was the end of anything the Tay Bridge Undertaking and the City of Dundee could expect in the way of celebration. They had their bridge, they could wait for it to become common-place, to watch with envy the celebrations that would surely take place when Mr Bouch had built his bridge over the Forth. The Dundee newspapers faced this inevitability generously. 'Everything about the Forth Bridge will be on a gigantic scale. The Tay Bridge – except in the manner of length – will be a mere trifle compared with the Forth Bridge.'

For the man who was responsible for these two great bridges there could be only one reward. Her Majesty, who appeared to have been impressed with Mr Bouch's modesty as much as with his bridge, let it be known that she was pleased to confer upon him a knighthood.

In Windsor Castle, at one o'clock on Thursday, 27 June 1879, Thomas Bouch accordingly received his reward, along with Henry Bessemer, Mr Justice Brown, and Major-General Henry Thuiller of the Indian Civil Service.

And now the doubts . . .

The Reverend Mr George Grubb, a member of the clergy at St George's Church, Dundee, made an odd discovery. When passing through the High Girders during a strong wind he was conscious of an extraordinary assault on his ears. It was, he said, an effect 'something similar to shocks of electricity, first in one ear and then in the other'. He amplified this, lest there be confusion. It was not electricity so much as 'something in the nature of a percussive effect'.

Others experienced this too, particularly if the windows of carriages were left open.

A number of businessmen who lived in Newport, and who travelled daily to Dundee by the bridge, reached the unsettling conclusion that trains were not keeping within the limit of 25 miles an hour set by General Hutchinson, but were rattling along at much higher speeds.

Mr William Robertson, an engineer and lately Provost of Dundee, was so alarmed that he went back to using the ferry, and this soon after he had bought a season ticket on the railway. Being a sensible man, however, he had first made sure that his suspicions were correct. He would sit in his first-class carriage with his watch in his hand and time the train across, particularly through the High Girders. In the evenings he would turn down the gaslight in his home at Newport and watch the trains crossing, but no longer for pleasure. He timed them once again.

It was his conclusion that some trains went through the High Girders in 50 seconds, which meant a speed of some 42 miles an hour.

His fellow-passengers did not find this concentration on his watch an odd matter, for most of them were studying their own with the same purpose.

Mr Alexander Hutchinson, an architect of Dundee who used the bridge frequently in the summer of 1879, found that the crossing from south to north rarely took longer than four and a half minutes, and once, to his intense alarm, it took no more than three and a half. He was also conscious of vertical oscillations in the High Girders, a movement which he considered to amount to as much as an inch.

Mr Thomas Baxter, a commission agent of Dundee, was also disturbed by the manner in which the struts of the High Girders flashed by the carriage windows. There was one particular day when he felt so much relief at having got off the bridge that he promptly changed his habits, returned to using the ferry, and never crossed the bridge again.

Ex-provost Robertson, being a man aware of his civic obligations, complained to James Smith, Station-master at Tay Bridge. Mr Smith listened to the complaint politely, but reminded Mr Robertson that it was not the duty of a station-master to caution the drivers about their speeds. 'With the greatest of civility,' however, he would refer the matter to them. He told Driver John Anderson to 'go cannily' for some of the gentlemen were complaining about the speeds, and Anderson smiled and said nothing, thinking, as he later explained, 'that the whole thing was perfect nonsense'.

Mr John Leng, managing proprietor and editor of the *Dundee Advertiser*, had a season ticket on the ferry, but in November 1878, he changed this for a season on the railway, commuting twice a day between his office in Dundee and his home at Newport.

He soon decided that the speeds travelled by the local trains were greatly in excess of 25 miles an hour when on the bridge. There was also, he said, 'a motion in the carriage not ordinarily felt on a level railway ... a prancing motion.' He too spoke to Station-master Smith about the speed of the trains, adding that 'some ladies were in a state of apprehension on the subject'.

Travelling over the firth by boat one evening, Leng met Henry Noble, Inspector of the bridge for the North British Railway. Leng button-holed him and complained about the speeds, and asked if his late employer, Sir Thomas Bouch, could not design some automatic register of speeds. Noble, that overworked man, said he would let Sir Thomas know, and perhaps he did.

There were other stories that alarmed these gentlemen, of the number of fallen bolts that were being found along the per-

manent way. It was said that down on the lower piers the bolts
were rusting through at an alarming rate.

The men who were painting the bridge knew this. David Pirie
and Peter Robertson once found three hundredweight of bolts
lying inside the lower booms. Some of them, of course, could
have been discarded there during the building, and in any case
the painters thought it none of their business.

Peter Donegany, a nineteen-year-old painter, found holes in
the girders too, but he had no knowledge to tell him whether
they should be there or not. John Milne, another painter, and
who was only sixteen, and employed to mix the paint, was
terrified of the bridge. Every time the train passed when he was
on the High Girders his stomach was sickened by the 'good dirl',
the vibration set up.

John Nelson, a mechanic turned by unemployment to painting the bridge, hated the vertical motion of the High Girders
when a train passed. And in a wind, as he clung to the iron in
the air, he noticed a lateral motion that left him 'pretty frightened and alarmed'.

John Gray, another painter, was to remember days when the
force of the wind was too great for him to work in the High
Girders. Then the bridge shook, he said, and he was too afraid to
go on it. He also remembered seeing rents in the iron of the piers
below the High Girders, but these meant nothing to him,
beyond the curious fact that a man could sink the whole blade
of a penknife in one of them.

Noble and his handful of men discovered some of these faults,
and some of them they did not. In any case Noble was overworked. He did, however, find a number of ties loose in the
cross-bracings. He did not tell Bouch, as he should have done,
but packed the gibs and cotters and paid for this out of his own
pocket. He also found some vertical cracks in several of the
columns, above the masonry. Bouch was told this time, and
the columns were braced with wrought-iron hoops.

The cement, that wonderful cement admired by Albert
Groethe, had burst the columns.

These things, however, the people did not know, and might

not have understood if they had. They were satisfied with the bridge. An aerial roadway to Fifeshire, it opened that beautiful land to the colour-starved workers of Dundee. On Sundays they took their ninepenny tickets at Tay Bridge Station, and travelled with their families to St Fort, picnicking there among the grass and the trees and the silent wind.

And if a few ministers preached darkly against this profane custom of running trains on the Sabbath, assuring the North British Railway that the Lord would seek vengeance in His own time, most people thought the bridge a wonderful thing, as indeed it was

# ACT TWO

*'Appalling Catastrophe at Dundee'*

# I

### 'There's mischief coming'

THE old Admiral, William Heriot Maitland Dougall, had an almost fanatical interest in two subjects. The first was of course the British Navy and its certain readiness for the moment the Russians would choose to revenge the Crimea. The second was the weather. He took daily, sometimes hourly readings of his barometer and aneroid. He studied General Reid's *Law of Storms*, and he kept a neat log of all his observations of the weather in the Firth of Tay.

His house was well situated for this purpose. He lived on the Fifeshire bank of Scotscraig, two hundred feet up, a mile and a quarter from the riverside, three from the Tay Bridge. From his windows he could look north across the Tayside Light, west to Errol and the Sidlaws, and east to the grey surge of the German Sea.

There had he lived for twenty-nine years. He had gone to sea in 1832, and had served without brilliance but with a single-minded devotion. Then, as he put it, 'I got wounded and was pensioned, and put on the shelf as a young captain.' The shelf was Scotscraig. Before he reached it, however, he had travelled much, and knew about the Indian and the Southern Seas, the Chinese and American too, and he knew what kind of wind made a hurricane and what kind did not.

It was quite early on the morning of Sunday, 28 December 1879, that he became uneasy about the weather. His servants watched him walking impatiently from the windows to his instruments, and thumbing the pages of the *Law of Storms*.

It had been a bad December, with storms and frosts prevailing. It had been a bad month all over Europe and had frozen the Seine at Paris. Yet to anyone but a man like the old Admiral

that particular Sunday had begun pleasantly. In the morning
and early afternoon there was a clear sky, and an absence of
wind that left a strange stillness in the air. Robert Kerr, the
assistant station-master at Tay Bridge, thought it a most gentle
day, and he hid his amusement when a minister stopped to talk
with him at the station gate, and to express his concern with the
weather. The minister said 'I do not doubt, Mr Kerr, that we
shall have a cyclone this day.'

The amateur astronomers of Tayside were indifferent to the
weather signs hidden in that clear, quiet atmosphere. They
watched a small eclipse of the moon which took place at 3.37
p.m., four minutes before sunset. The moon itself was scarcely
above the horizon, and for a while the view of the eclipse was
splendid. But shortly after four o'clock it began to rain. At sixteen minutes past four, full moon and at approximately the
middle of the eclipse, the rain was quite heavy.

Heavy enough to irritate and alarm the Admiral as he trudged
from church beneath his umbrella. There was no wind, and the
noise of the rain on the earth was like muted applause. When
he reached his house Admiral Dougall closed his umbrella,
thrust it into the hall-stand, and went to his barometer. There
had been a sharp fall from 29.40 to 28.80. He asked if the instrument had been touched, and his servants said no. He compared
it with the aneroid and the figures corresponded.

He went to the door of his conservatory and looked across his
garden. In the dusk the trees and shrubs were bending with the
weight of the rain, particularly the branches of a fine old
walnut tree. The Admiral was suddenly worried about this tree,
and its power to withstand a heavy wind. He saw his gardener
moving about the shrubs, and he called out 'There's mischief
coming!'

He suddenly remembered the terrible gale of October 1860,
which had swept through his property insanely, uprooting trees
and tossing chimney-cairns about like leaves.

He went inside and brought his log to date. He noted that at 5
p.m. the wind changed to the westward. Then it changed three
points more to the westward and braced up into a heavy gale.

The bridge from the south in 1877. 'A train could be driven across whenever the directors of the Undertaking wished.' (*Photo by Valentine,
Dundee*)

*Above* The first columns on the south bank.
*Below* The pontoons on which the piers were floated out to their positions.

*Above* 'Seventy men and boys began to build the bridge from a land abutment on the south bank. In the beginning the piers were built in two parts, two cylinders of wrought iron filled with a lining of brick-work up to the level of low water, with an opening in the centre. They were carried out and sunk to their positions on the river bed.'

*Below* How the girders were floated out to the bridge from Wormit.

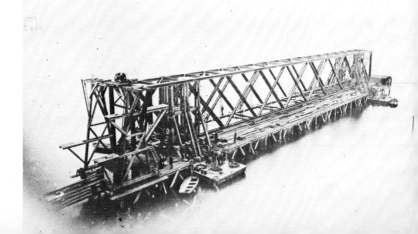

*Above* The Tay bridge from the north.
*Below* A section of the south side of the bridge.

The ferry-boat *Dundee* visited the ruins on the night of the disaster. 'They saw twelve black stumps where the river leaped and played. And above the stumps there was nothing. Some of the gentlemen wept.'

Diving operations in search of the wreck of the train.

The northern end of the gap. From here, southward, there was nothing for over a thousand yards. It was to this point that Foreman James Roberts crawled on the night of the disaster and lay on his belly. The broken rails can be seen, wrenched to the east.

These Tickets were Collected at St Fort Station, on 28th December, 1879, by Robert Morris, Agent; Wm. Friend, Ticket Collector; and Alex. Inglis, Porter, from the Passengers who lost their lives by the Fall of the Tay Bridge.

'Until Station-agent Robert Morris came over the Tay from St Fort the city grieved for three hundred dead. In his pocket Morris carried the tickets which he and his staff had collected ...' The tickets were later framed with photographs of the Company's dead. Top left and reading clockwise: Driver Mitchell, Stoker Marshall, Guards Johnson and Macbeath. *(Photo by Valentine, Dundee)*

'This was the eighth day, and, if the whalers were to be believed, the lost dead would now rise to the surface for Christian burial.' (*Photo by Valentine, Dundee*)

The Admiral went to the window and looked eastward to the darkness hiding the German Sea. He noticed the extreme difference between the fury of the squalls and the peacefulness of the lulls between them. They awakened old memories, and he looked out towards the sea again and said 'What a trying gale for the poor fellows of those ships which haven't strength to make continual sail in a roll. When they roll heavily to windward they get struck and swept by coming seas.'

He estimated the wind-force of the squalls. He thought that it must be between 75 and 78. All the windows in his house were rattling, and he was afraid that they would be blown in.

On board the *Mars*, out in the Tay, Captain Scott had also noticed the alarming drop in the glass. There was a rapid fall from noon until seven o'clock. Quite early in the afternoon he called along to have everything made fast and snug. A Naval man, with much service behind him, Captain Scott had long ago learnt to assess the force of a gale by numbers, from one to a maximum of 12. He estimated that this gale coming down the firth was Force 10 to 11. It was six years since there had been a wind as strong as this on the Tay. It was almost as bad as the Force 12 gale that had hit his ship in the mouth of the Plate many years before. His memory went on from this incident to recall the gales he had experienced in the China Seas, and the thought disturbed him deeply.

Seaman-Instructor High McMahon was keeping the log of the *Mars*. He recorded a gale force of 10 to 11, something he had never known before. He said so to the Gunnery Instructor, Edward Batsworth, who was sharing the watch. Batsworth recorded the blow of the wind. At four o'clock – west-south-west. At five o'clock – west-south-west. At six o'clock the same, and at seven too.

Over in Westfield Cottage, on Magdalen Green, a retired businessman called Charles Clark kept a daily record of the weather 'for private amusement and information'. For 14 of the 52 years he had lived in the cottage he had kept his record as fully as possible. It was his custom to assess wind force from 0 to 6. This Sunday night he wrote 6 in the wind column of his record. From nine in the morning until late evening he marked the fall of the barometer. At five p.m. he rose from his tea to record the lowest point of its fall.

Captain John Grieg, Superintendent of the Lights at Tayport, was on shore duty. He was in the West Tower, below Spears Hill, and at 5 p.m. he climbed to the lantern 67 feet above sealevel to watch the lamp being lit. The whole fabric of the tower was vibrating continuously, like a leaf held fast to a branch in a steady wind. Captain Grieg went home to tea, very uneasy in mind.

By 5.30 the gale was punishing Dundee. Above its eldritch howling there was the continual clatter of falling tiles, the sudden crack and debris-roll of collapsing chimneys. The congregation in Ward's Chapel sat forward on the edges of their seats, scarcely listening to Mr Short's sermon, but waiting for each new sound of falling cairns. This, as one of them later described it, was like the roll of iron plates.

At the top of Commercial Street a photographic booth suddenly exploded. Its large window was blown out and flung down the street, scattering a hail of glass. The planks and slates slapped themselves madly against the kerbs and the walls.

A large wooden board, about 30 feet long and 5 feet deep, was torn from the top of Lamb's Hotel and thrown to the middle of Reform Street. Along the shore below the Esplanade the wind ripped off the roofs of the bathing huts one by one and either smashed them against the thick white wall, or whirled them out into the darkness of the river. An attic roof in Kinloch Street was stripped of its tiles, lathes and plaster, and the rain and the wind beat in on a screaming tweeny maid. Heavy stones were withdrawn from the walls of a house in Wolseley Street, and all over the city the shutters banged and banged until they tore themselves from their hinges and rolled along the kerbs like scraps of paper.

The gale was roaring the whole length of Tayside, hitting Lochee, Arbroath, Colliston, Kirriemuir and Montrose. People who were walking abroad in Dundee, returning from church or departing for it, kept close to the walls to avoid the flying tiles.

Chimney cairns were whirling about, leaping and capering in the middle of the roads beneath the dim gaslight. There was scarcely any halt in the unearthly noise of toppling masonry.

The Reverend George Grubb arrived at Tay Bridge Station on the 6.10 from Newport. It was the last train but one to be expected from the south that night. The minister was considerably shaken. More than ever before had he been conscious of that curious percussive effect as the train passed through the High Girders. One of his fellow passengers had opened a window on the west side because he wished to demonstrate his contention that the wind, passing through the carriages, set up electrical shock waves. The Reverend Mr Grubb said that he had himself experienced this, and would be obliged if the gentleman closed the window. He looked out of the east window and was not at all comforted by the sight of an angry river, seen momentarily in the moonlight.

The guard of the train that carried Mr Grubb across was Robert Shand. Arriving at Tay Bridge Station he went forward to speak to Alexander Kennedy, the driver. He seemed much shaken, and he said (although he afterwards denied saying it) 'I'd not go across the bridge again tonight for £500. My coach was lifted from the rails and streaks of fire came from it.'

Sparks had come from the wheels in the middle of the train, too, and when he saw them Shand put on his brake, but this made no difference and soon the sparks flowered along the wheels of all the carriages. Shand thought that an axle had broken, and he leant from the window of the brake van and waved a red lantern towards the engine. Kennedy did not see it.

Kennedy and Shand stood on the platform at Tay Bridge Station arguing about this, with the driver saying that sparks always came from the wheels on the bridge, and Shand saying no, the force of the wind had driven the wheels against the rails.

Station-master James Smith had no reason to be on duty that night, but shortly after six o'clock a locomotive foreman came running to his house, calling 'Mr Smith, there's a great gale blowing the wagons along the viaduct!'

This was so extraordinary a claim that Mr Smith refused to

believe it, but he put on a heavy top-coat and went down to the yards. He found that the foreman was correct. The wind had blown three wagons four hundred yards up an ascending gradient. Each wagon was full of coal, and each must have weighed ten tons.

With two labourers Mr Smith scotched up the wagons so that they would be blown no further, and he hurried on to the station. As he walked along the platform his feet scuffled a thick layer of broken glass that had been blown from the roof. The glass was still flying through the air, and he walked to his office with his hands before his face.

He called for the station inspector and he said 'Mr Caird, please shut the exit gates at Union Street Bridge and keep the public from the station. When the Edinburgh train comes in don't let the passengers out that way for the glass is blowing about badly.'

William Robertson had been Harbour Master at Dundee for eight years. On Sunday evenings he always went to church with his wife, but this evening the noise of the gale was so terrifying that he thought he should first visit his office at the docks. He tried to force a way against the wind at an exposed corner near the Customs House, and at last gave up the attempt. He went home and told Mrs Robertson that he would go alone to church.

Shortly after seven, as he sat in the church, 'there was something very strange took place, like as if the side of the building, or some of the roofing, or something had given way'. For a time the noise halted the minister in his sermon, and even when he began to speak again none of the congregation could hear him, so great was the noise of the wind. 'Like something rolling along the roof,' Robertson thought.

In his father's house at Magdalen Green young Alexander Maxwell was entertaining friends. They were deliciously thrilled by the storm, by the chandelier shaking and tinkling musically above their heads, by the roll and crash of chimney cairns outside. They were young, and violence excited them tremendously. A young man called William Millar said why should they not draw back the curtains, and wait for the Edinburgh train to cross the bridge?

So the gaslight was turned down, and the curtains were pulled back, and the young people drew their chairs up to the window.

In another house along the Green, George Clark and his brother William also drew back their curtains to watch the train cross. So did others, here and there across the city, wherever the windows faced the Bridge of Tay. In Newport, too, ex-Provost Robertson was also at his villa window, watching the river.

At seven o'clock the storm reached its zenith. Captain Scott took a barometer reading aboard the *Mars* and logged it as 29.00. He looked anxiously westward into the gale and felt thankful he was not at sea.

At five minutes past seven a small turret was blown from St Peter's church, Dundee, to sail negligently through the air before it fell to the roadway and burst into dust.

And at ten minutes past seven Admiral Dougall went to his window at Scotscraig and looked out through the black panes and the distortion of the rain. He could see very little except the dark, writhing shadows of the shrubs and the trees. He had just been reading the General's book on storms again, and recalling to his mind that the force of the most violent hurricane was perhaps one hundred miles an hour. The force of these gusts that were now mauling his garden, he thought, must be seventy-eight, which was very bad for a country so far removed from the aerial violence of the China Seas.

He thought sadly of his trees. He knew that because their roots were inclined to shoot out of the ground in the direction of the prevailing wind (south by east at Scotscraig) they should better withstand a westerly gale like this. But still he was uneasy, and he was particularly worried about his walnut tree, 'many hundreds of years old'.

He regretted that his health and his age no longer made it wise for him to go out after dark in foul weather, for he greatly wished to be with his beloved tree at this moment. In the snatches of moonlight he could see broken branches on the grass, 'as if they had been wounded by round-shot'.

Then his gardener came into the conservatory, closing the door behind him, and wiping the rain from his face before he spoke to the Admiral.

He said that the walnut tree was down, it had 'all gone smash', nothing but the stump left, and two low branches on the weather side.

This happened at twenty minutes past seven o'clock, and Admiral Dougall was to remember the time, for it was the exact moment, as near as anybody could tell, that the High Girders fell into the Tay.

# II

*'The train drives on in moonlight grey,
But will it cross the Bridge o' Tay?'*

THERE was little rail traffic in Scotland on Sundays. No company closed its lines now, as did the Edinburgh and Glasgow in the old days, thus encouraging the vice of alcoholism, but the traffic was kept to a minimum. Even this did not satisfy the Sabbatarians, who preached frequently and at length on the railway companies' contempt for the Lord's Day.

Every Sunday the mail train ran from Dundee to Burntisland and back. It left Tay Station at 1.30 p.m., and began its journey back at 5.20 p.m., having picked up the ferry passengers who came across the Forth from Edinburgh. It arrived in Dundee shortly before seven-thirty.

The regular driver of this train was David Mitchell, a sober, careful man with a gentle face and a beard that grew along the line of his jaw only, in the fashion of that day. He had previously driven trains between Tayport and Burntisland, but upon the opening of the bridge he moved his wife and family (there were three boys and two girls, all under ten) to Dundee. He had a great pride in his work, and a love of the engines he drove. His moleskin trousers were always spotlessly white when he began his run, and he was known to be a genial, equable man. He was deeply fond of his children.

His stoker was John Marshall, a young man of twenty-four who had been with the North British for eight years and who was unmarried. He was tall and thin, with long arms and a dark mane of hair. Because he was a bachelor he frequently spent his free evenings with the Mitchell family, and there was a strong friendship between the two men. Marshall's greatest possession was a silver watch that kept accurate time, as a railwayman's watch should, and he kept it in his breast pocket wrapped in cotton waste.

On Sunday, 28 December 1879, the Drummond tank engine which normally pulled the mail train had broken down, and in its place Mitchell was given the spare engine at Dundee, a Wheatley bogie, Number 224.

She had been built at Cowlairs in 1871, one of the first two engines to be built of the Standard British 4–4–o type, having 17-inch cylinders with a 24-inch stroke. She had 6 feet 6 inch driving wheels that turned under gracefully-perforated hoods, and she had a Westinghouse brake as well as two handbrakes.

She was a stumpy little thing, but quaintly impressive. Her predecessors on the old North British line had sometimes been painted in tartan, but No. 224 was olive-green in body and bright in brass, with thin red lines emphasizing her curves and angles. But for a narrow cowling her footplate was open to the weather. She was 27 feet 6 inches long and she weighed 34 tons 12 cwts.

The train she pulled that Sunday night consisted of five passenger coaches and a brake van. None of the carriages was very new. Some were still painted in red, the dark claret of the line, but at least one was made of varnished teak panels.

The first carriage, No. 579, was four-wheeled, having five doors on either side and two ventilators on its roof. It was labelled 'N.B.R. THIRD CLASS.' It weighed 8 tons 8 cwts. The second carriage, No. 414, of more comfortable build, had six wheels, five doors, five ventilators, and was labelled 'N.B.R. FIRST CLASS.' It weighed 14 tons 5 cwts. Then another four-wheeled third-class carriage, No. 629, weighing the same as the first. The fourth carriage was third class again, having five ventilators and weighing 9 tons 16 cwts. It was No. 650. The last of the passenger accommodation was a small second-class carriage, No. 138, with four doors and two ventilators. It weighed only 5 tons 19 cwts.

The brake van, occupied that Sunday evening by a bearded, taciturn guard called David Macbeath, was 26 feet 2 inches long and weighed 8 tons 9 cwts unloaded, but on the night of the

Great Storm it was carrying 46 mail-bags in addition to other luggage.

The length of the whole train was almost 225 feet, and its weight without passengers was 114 tons 14 cwts. With its wide couplings, tall smoke-stack on the jaunty engine, with its comic ventilator cowlings and bright colours, it could look, from a distance, like a toy train circumnavigating the furniture of a drawing-room.

The coaches were upholstered in varying hues according to age, but the predominant colour was that dark plum-red which railway companies everywhere have found most resistant to stains and most conducive to passenger melancholy. The doors of the first-class compartments were handsomely padded on the inside. There were arm-rests, laced antimacassars, hassocks, foot-warmers, head-cushions. All coaches were lit by brass and iron lanterns that perpetuated the Gothic taste of the Great Exhibition.

At 5.20 p.m., in the cold darkness and the strong south-westerly wind, No. 224 pulled her train out of Burntisland from the north. There were few passengers aboard, a score or so travelling up to Dundee from Edinburgh, but as she stopped on her way through Fife, at Ladybank, at Cupar, at Leuchars and at St Fort, she would pick up others.

At Ladybank, for example, a gentleman tugged open the door of a first-class compartment, letting in whorls of steam and sulphur fumes. He tossed his bag inside and climbed in after it. He was flustered and indignant. His name was William Henry Benyon and he was an Englishman aged thirty-nine. As people will when they have luckily avoided an awkward mistake while travelling, he was anxious to talk to the passenger already in the compartment.

Mr Benyon was a remarkably well-dressed man. He wore a diamond ring, a plain buckle ring, a Masonic scarf pin, a valuable gold watch and a heavy Albert with great golden links. And, although his fellow-passenger could not know this, he had something between £80 and £100 in banknotes in his pocketbook.

He was, he said, the director of a fine art and lithography company in Cheltenham. He and his Scottish representative had sat in the refreshment room at Waverley Station earlier that afternoon trying to decide which of them should make this business trip to Dundee. In the end Benyon had decided to go, but so confused had he become as a result of the discussion that when he arrived at Burntisland he boarded a train for Perth, instead of waiting for the 5.20 to Dundee.

He considered it a stroke of great luck that while he was sitting in his compartment at Ladybank a porter passed the window calling 'Perth!' Otherwise, he said, he would never have reached Dundee that night.

His fellow-passenger alighted at Leuchars, and thus took with him this fragmentary memory of the last hour in the life of Mr William Henry Benyon, who had nearly missed his train.

In a third-class carriage sat Ann Cruickshank, aged fifty-three, spinster and housemaid to Lady Baxter of Kilmaron. She was travelling with her niece, Eliza Smart, another of her ladyship's maids. Ann Cruickshank was going to comfort a sick friend at Broughty Ferry, but Eliza had been given a few days holiday and was scarcely able to sit still in the thought that her sweetheart, George Johnston, would be waiting to join the train and her at St Fort.

Ann Cruickshank felt the cold badly. She had wrapped and tied a heavy scarf about her throat, and she was dressed in thick black clothes, black petticoats, black skirt, black coat and black bonnet. She looked, as many women of her age looked, a loyal replica of the old Queen. She carried no reticule. Her handkerchief, her handful of copper and silver, her ticket to Broughty Ferry, were in the pockets of her long black jacket.

She was in a petulant mood. It had been her intention to catch an earlier train, but Lady Baxter's coachman, who was to have driven them to the station, had overslept and they had missed the train.

William Threlfell, who was eighteen and a confectioner's apprentice at Union Street, Dundee, was travelling home from Edinburgh where he had been visiting his brother, a trooper in the Enniskillen Dragoons. He was a devout and studious boy, much given to reading the scriptures and with a fondness for singing in the choir. He had a hymn-book in one pocket of his jacket, and in the other a single shilling and his ticket.

Walter Ness, returning from a visit to friends at Auchter-muchty, was a foreman saddler. He was also a valued member of the Dundee Artillery Volunteers, who were later to bury him with full military honours.

John Scott, aged twenty-six, and fresh from the other side of the world, had been discharged from his ship at Hartlepool on Christmas Eve. He was now on his way home to Dundee, with silver American dollars ringing in his pocket.

In another third-class carriage, his jacket buttoned to his throat against the cold, sat David Neish, schoolmaster and regis-trar of Lochee. He was returning from a Sunday visit to friends at Kirkcaldy, and his favourite daughter Bella was with him. She was five years old, with large brown eyes and soft dark hair. Her little legs, in their high-buttoned boots, stuck out over the edge of the seat. She wore a pill-box hat decorated with crêpe feathers, and she wore bright tartan revers and cuffs on her jacket. A quiet child, she was sometimes so immobile that she looked like a doll.

William Macdonald was also travelling with his child. He was forty-one, a sawmiller who lived at Blackness Road in Dundee, and had taken his boy Davie to see friends in Fife. Davie was eleven, but small for his age and dark. He wore a check tweed suit, his Sunday suit of which he was very proud, a check wincey shirt, brown-ribbed stockings, and a mourning cap (for there was a death in the family). He was delighted by the thought that he was to cross the Tay for the second time in one day. He sat close to the window so that he might see the lights on the river.

Mr Macdonald was wearing a mourning tie. On his waistcoat was a gold Albert joining a silver watch to a silver seal. In his pocket was his pipe, and with it a whistle, a knife, a watchkey, two handkerchiefs and a purse containing 7s. 1½d.

William Jack, a young grocer of Dundee, was also in mourning, with a band of crêpe on his arm, and he was not making this journey for pleasure. His sister had been buried a week before, and he was returning from a visit of comfort to his mother.

This atmosphere of death touched the train with dramatic irony that night. There were black mourning clothes on a young ploughman called James Crichton, and on a forester called William Peebles.

Crichton had a double-cased silver watch in his waistcoat pocket. It had belonged to his father, who had been buried that afternoon in a Downfield kirkyard while the young man watched. Crichton worked on a farm at Mains of Fintry and his employer, Mr Bell, had told him that he need not return before Monday. But Crichton was a diligent and conscientious youth, and now the sole supporter of a mother and two sisters, so he decided to come back on the Sunday train.

William Peebles had been to his father's funeral, too. And he had also decided to take this train and not one later. At Corrimony, where he was well esteemed, he was a forester. There was a gun licence in his pocket, and also his day-book neatly entered to date. He had greatly loved his father.

Robert Watson boarded the train at Cupar and was no doubt glad to be going home. It had been a long day, and travelling with two high-spirited young boys, no matter how lovable, was exhausting. The boys were his sons, Robert aged six, and David aged nine. Mrs Watson had opposed her husband's proposal to take the boys to see Fifeshire friends that Sunday, and had asked him to postpone the visit until the New Year. But the boys had been excited by the thought of crossing the Tay, and Watson had not wished to disappoint them once he had given his promise.

He was a gentle and kindly man, a man much moved by the emotions or the suffering of others. Of his four brothers one was totally blind, and for this blind man Robert Watson had a great love. It was a practical love, in that he gave active support to the Dundee Blind Institute. In his pocket was a programme of a concert recently given in aid of charity.

John Sharp, a joiner of Commercial Street in Dundee, sat alone in his compartment, very tired. He had spent Sunday with friends at St Andrews, and had spent it so well that he almost agreed when they pressed him to stay overnight. But in the end he decided against it, and had walked all the way through the rain from St Andrews to Leuchars to catch the last train.

Between David Cunningham and Robert Fowlis there was no thought of bereavement, of weariness, of anything but the great pleasure they found in each other's company. They had been friends since childhood. They lodged together at the same boarding-house in Dundee, and there was little in their happily ordinary lives that these young men did not do together, from working to playing, except fall in love. Robert Fowlis was in love. In his jacket was a letter from his sweetheart.

At Leuchars, shortly before seven o'clock, George Ness, a young cleaner in the locomotive shed at Tay Bridge Station, walked down the platform and joined his friends Mitchell and Marshall on the engine, and rode with them there to their death.

At Leuchars, too, Mr William Linskill, a gentleman travelling first class, prepared to alight and to travel on by carriage to St Andrews where his friend the Dean was expecting him. He leant from the window into the steam and the turbid lamp-light, calling to a porter whom he knew. 'Is there a carriage here for me?' he said. The porter shook his head and Mr Linskill pulled up the strap of the window and sat down again, much discontented. He said to his fellow-passenger, who was, of course, Mr Benyon, that if the carriage were not there then he would travel on to Dundee and abandon his intention of visiting the Dean. At that moment the porter rapped on the window 'Your carriage is here now, Mr Linskill!'

So Mr Linskill said goodnight to the gentleman from Cheltenham and alighted. For some long time afterwards, being a humble man, he was to wonder why the Almighty had chosen to save him and not Mr Benyon.

Leaving Leuchars northwards the train began to feel the periphery of the great gale that was driving down the Firth of Tay. The wind beat down the smoke from its stack, rattled the windows of the carriages, whistling in through ventilators and cracks. The passengers drew their coats tighter about them. There were now over sixty men, women and children riding on the train.

There was Robert Syme, aged twenty-two, recently married and a clerk at the Royal Hotel, a keen and ambitious young man who had been visiting his father in Edinburgh. There was 'a youth of great promise', David Watson, also twenty-two, who had been visiting friends in Fife, and he did not know that travelling on this train with him was a little boy of his own name. There was John Lawson, who was lighter in heart than he had been for many months, for he had been out of work a long time and had just obtained work as a plasterer. He had given himself a visit to Fifeshire as a small celebration of his good fortune.

In the second-class coach at the rear of the train sat a young timber merchant's clerk, James Leslie. He, too, had been visiting friends in Fifeshire, and because he found rail journeys at night, particularly in winter, greatly tedious he always took a book with him to read.

This night it was a copy of Longfellow's poems, a prize awarded him for Reading at Dundee High School in 1871. He read it in the flickering lantern-light until, as the train neared the Tay, he closed it and placed it in his pocket.

In another second-class compartment Archibald Bain sat with his sister Jessie. He was a farmer of Balgay and the local agent for the sale of manures. He was a proud man, and a successful man in a modest way, with golden sovereigns in his pocket, and a silver watch and chain at his waist. He wore a heavy ulster and a warm scarf, and his face was red and full with the health of open air and good living.

Jessie was a pretty little girl much admired by the young men around Balgay, and much pleased by their admiration. She was in love, however, and in the pocket of her muff she carried a warm letter from the young man she hoped to marry. She carried another letter too, and the fact that she still had it with her was greatly vexing. For it was one she had written to her father a day or so before, and had forgotten to post.

It was nearly seven o'clock when No. 224 panted up the vale of Motray Water towards St Fort. The rain was hitting her now, hissing into the open cab, and striking against the windows of the carriages like handfuls of gravel. She made her last crossing of the Water, ran smartly under the Kilmany road bridge and pulled up at the station at five minutes past seven. Station-agent Robert Morris snapped the case of his watch with satisfaction. The train was on time.

St Fort was not then, any more than it is now, a town or a village, but just a station lying pleasantly in the low ground between Newton Hill and Links Wood, a restful spot in summer, a green saucer holding the heat of the sun and the lingering hum of insects. That Sunday night, however, it was feeling the edge of a gale. The orange flames of the lamps, in their quaintly decked cowlings, were jumping nervously. Rain dripped from the station roof, or was whipped along almost parallel with the earth.

George Johnston, his head butting the wind, ran along the platform, looking through the steamed windows of each third-class carriage, searching for the sweet face of Eliza Smart. He had been spending the day with his father, who was a keeper on the St Fort estate, but he had left early, believing, as all anxious lovers believe, that there is a conspiracy among all public transport companies to bedevil the course of love by altering their time-tables.

At last he found Eliza and climbed in to join her, no doubt resigning himself to the fact that so long as the spinster was with them they could do no more than hold hands under the skirts of his coat.

It was the custom, with such trains as this, and at such times, for the staff of St Fort to collect the tickets of all passengers terminating their journey at Dundee. And so, his head and shoulders covered by oil-skin, Robert Morris opened the doors of the last two coaches, calling into the wind and the rain 'Tickets, please!'

William Friend, ticket collector, Alexander Ingles, porter, similarly collected tickets from the other carriages. Afterwards

Ingles remembered that in one carriage a man had smiled at him across the cradled head of a sleeping child, and that there had been another boy asleep on the seat.

The last ticket collected, the three men stood together in the centre of the platform, while at the rear of the train, one foot on and one foot off the step of the brake van, Guard David Macbeath slapped the shutter of his lamp to green and blew his shrill whistle into the noise of the gale. He stepped inside the van and swung the door behind him just as the van passed the station staff. They saw the white flash of his hand in salute, and then the window went up with a snap.

Morris returned to the warmth of his office to sort the tickets. He and the other two men had collected 57. Ten or eleven passengers travelling on beyond Dundee, he remembered, had retained theirs. There had also been two season-ticket holders.

Thus, the little train, swinging through the cuttings on the Peacehill bend north-east to Wormit, was carrying 69 or 70 passengers. In addition there were five of the company's servants – Driver Mitchell and his stoker Marshall, Guard Macbeath and two other guards. These last two men were not on duty but were keeping Macbeath company in the brake van as they travelled to work.

Seventy-five men, women and children on the 5.20 from Burntisland, engine 224.

Five minutes after leaving St Fort the train reached the Wormit signal box where Signalman Barclay was waiting. He walked alongside the engine for a few paces and handed the baton to Marshall.

And then the train drove on to the Tay Bridge and into the storm.

# III

'O horror! The train and the bridge are over
Into the depths of the wintry wave!'

IN the upstairs room of the Maxwell house along Magdalen
Green young Alexander and his friends had grown weary of
their watch.

They had been waiting a long time. There was nothing to be
seen from the window but the darkness and the rain in runnels
on the glass. Alexander suggested that they draw the curtains
and sit by the fire once more to tell stories and sing songs, but
William Millar insisted that they waited. He said that he wished
to see the train cross the bridge and he intended to see the train
cross the bridge. He carried them with him and they decided to
wait a little longer.

Shortly after seven o'clock they saw the lights of the train as
it entered upon the bridge, a dim, uncertain glimmer far away.
Alexander watched the signal light to the north of the High
Girders. It was flickering and he wondered if the lamp had set
fire to its mounting. Then he took his eyes from it and watched
the approach of the train. He watched until it entered the High
Girders and then he saw one, two, three great flashes of light
that lasted long enough for him to see the fretwork of iron, or
think he saw it. It was his opinion that these flashes occurred *in
front* of the train, and he always maintained that this was so.

William Millar, however, believed that the flashes came from
the train itself, and when he saw them he turned to his friends
and said jocularly that the fireman must be in a hurry to get
home for he was drawing his fire already, and was throwing the
coals into the river.

It was not easy to see anything with great certainty, for one
moment there would be a scud of cloud across the moon and

the next moment the scene would be clear in the pallid light. William stood up and moved close to the window. He saw a white flash against the bridge. 'They're blowing steam, now,' he said, and scarcely had he said this than he shouted in a vastly altered tone.

'*The bridge is doon!*'

But he was known to be a great joker, and his friends laughed at him. They slapped his back, and poked their fingers in his ribs. He shook himself away from them and flung wide his arms. He said '*The bridge is doon!*'

Old Mr Maxwell, who had come into the room earlier, was annoyed by what he considered to be Millar's bad taste. 'Oh, Wull,' he said, 'Wull, w'ye pairseest in saying it?'

But William Millar did so persist, and Mr Maxwell said irritably to his son 'Sandy, awa' and get your telescope.'

The instrument was brought and focused on the bridge just at that moment when the moon came out strongly, and remained out for some minutes, as if the storm wished to boast of its work. Mr Maxwell looked and silently handed the telescope to the boys. He had seen a gap in the bridge a thousand yards long. He had seen the black stumps sticking from the river. He had seen the water from the main spraying up into a great white fern and falling to the east.

'Oh, Wull,' he said, 'I take back every word I said tae ye!'

In their home at Magdalen Point, opposite the north signal cabin, the brothers George and William Clark had also been watching the storm and the bridge. George, who had travelled much in the Far East, said frequently that this night reminded him of a hurricane and he feared for the train. They watched the night intently, and it was while George had turned away to relieve the strain on his eyes that William cried out 'Look at the fire! The train's over the bridge!'

He had seen the three flashes of light and he had seen the great cloud of spray or steam.

The brothers went up to the observatory at the top of the house where they kept a large telescope, but it could not be used without opening the windows, and the wind was too strong for that. So they held their faces close to the panes and stared out, seeing nothing but the blackness of the night.

Mr Phin, the grocer of Perth Road, was also at his window watching the bridge with friends. He saw the train enter the bridge, he saw the flickering lights of the carriages, and then he saw 'two fearful volumes of flame'.

'Did ye see that?' he said. 'Did ye see that? The bridge is down.'

Mr William Robertson, watching from the window of his home at Newport, saw *two* columns of spray leap up suddenly from the waters below the High Girders, and then he saw nothing but darkness. Even when the moon came out the rain was too thick, the distance too far for him to see more.

Little Jamie Norval, returning from Lindsay Street Congregational Church with his father, shivered with an excitement that was sometimes fear and sometimes pleasure. The wind was strong along Nethergate and the man and boy crept cautiously by the lee of a high wall. Jamie was delighted by the sight of people being blown about like tops when they tried to cross the road. At last he and his father reached a low wall at the top of Seabraes and there they halted to catch their breath. They looked out to the bridge.

'Father,' said Jamie suddenly, 'was that no' lightning?'

'I don't think so,' said Mr Norval, in a strange, unnatural tone which Jamie was to remember even fifty years later. 'I don't think so. It was too low down on the water.'

Across the river Signalman Barclay, with the breath hot in his chest, his feet stumbling on the track, was running down the line to Newport, shouting 'The bridge is doon!' to every shadow he passed. His friend James Watt ran to St Fort, and when he reached the little station he told Station-agent Morris that the Tay Bridge had fallen, and then he ran on in the darkness to Leuchars. He ran two miles to St Fort, and more than four miles from there to Leuchars carrying the terrible news.

On the north bank, in his signal cabin at Magdalen Point, Henry Somerville waited uneasily. For over an hour his box had been shaking, and his ears were tired of the whistle of the wind, the hysterical rattling of door and windows. The gale pushed and thumped and sucked at every plank.

At 7.13 p.m. he received Barclay's signal that the train was on the bridge and he acknowledged it. In five minutes the 5.20 should pass his box, and he was ready to go down to collect the baton. He waited for five minutes, and he waited nine more until it was almost seven-thirty, and being a man of little imagination he could think of no explanation for the delay. He left the box and went down to the boarding, standing there, staring along the line of the bridge, and frowning. He saw nothing but one red signal light, hanging in the sky a thousand yards away.

It was there, and suddenly it was there no longer.

Mr James Black Lawson was a successful wine merchant who lived on the eastern perimeter of Magdalen Green. He saw the bridge fall.

Early in the evening he had been at his window, watching the river running high and blowing into foam. He became so fascinated by the sight that he left his house to stand on the embankment, and there he was joined by his friend Mr Smart. They saw the flashes, the spray of water.

Lawson said 'There is a train into the river!'

They ran across the Green, through the Caledonian Railway Yard to the shelter of the southernmost of the great piers. There they halted and looked at the river, but could see nothing. A shadow moved in the darkness towards them. It was an acquaintance, Mr Clark, and he said 'Something is terribly wrong, gentlemen.'

They moved under the bridge until they came below Somerville's cabin, looking up to the faint yellow light of it, and calling out to the signalman many times. At last Somerville's pale face peered over the rail of the boarding.

'Is there a train due on the bridge?' shouted Lawson. Somerville nodded. 'Then I am afraid it is in the river.'

Lawson and his friends ran eastward along the Esplanade, and walked when they no longer had the breath to run. People were coming down from the city, and standing in little groups, wrapped in shawls, or with heads bent under low-pulled bonnets. They asked questions of each other and scarcely waited for the answers. They snatched at Mr Lawson's sleeve as he went by, but he shook himself free and shouted to Clark to carry the news to the *Advertiser* office. He would go to the station.

Peter Barron, a carriage inspector for the Caledonian Railway, lived at Balgay Lodge on the Blackness Road. That Sunday evening, from dusk almost, he stood nervously at his front window, watching his chimney cairns come down into his garden like bursting grenades. He went out, shortly after seven, to shutter a window, and before he returned he decided to cross the road to look at the bridge. The roadway was only 20 feet in breadth, but it took him several minutes to cross it against the wind.

He was the only man that night who clearly saw what happened, or who said he saw what happened. He saw, or said he saw, first one girder and then another break free from the piers and fall into the water. He did not just see lights and *know* that they must have come from a falling span, he *saw* the High Girders fall. Or said he saw.

'As near as I could guess in my mind it would have been about the first girder or the second girder upon the large girders. I just immediately got nervous at once, and I rubbed my eyes . . . In a second or two I saw another lump going, and just at that time I saw the southernmost part of the high girder, I saw a blink of light and the blink of light had cleared away.

'The moon was shining as clear as could be on the river, and I saw the large piers from end to end.'

He ran inside, he said (and this was at the official Inquiry), to tell his family. Then he ran out again to the road and there met his friend Henry Gourlay, a boat-builder.

He said he told Gourlay that he had seen the girders fall, but this Gourlay later denied, and seemed angry that Barron should make the claim. That night the storm seems not only to have destroyed a bridge, but also the friendship between Peter Barron and Henry Gourlay.

At Tay Bridge Station James Smith was standing on the western end of the platform and staring towards the bridge. He could see little but the dying gleam of the rails, the red and green pricks of the signal lamps. It was well beyond half-past seven and the signals were still set for the train. They had been so for many minutes, and Station-master Smith knew what this meant. The train had entered upon the bridge but had not left it. This was inexplicable.

Behind Smith was a silent group of station staff, shielding their faces from the glass that was still whirring through the air. One of these was Robert Shand, guard of the last train to cross the bridge. Smith called out to him, and asked him to telegraph Barclay at Wormit. Shand went away, and he came back in three minutes. 'There is no reply, Mr Smith,' he said.

Smith returned to his office, and it was there that Lawson and Smart found him. Emotion and exhaustion made it difficult for Lawson to speak.

'We have seen fire falling from the bridge, Mr Smith. We're very much afraid it's down!'

Smith stood up and grasped Lawson's arm. 'Please, gentlemen, tell nobody. There'll be great anxiety.'

Lawson said 'I must tell the harbour-master. A boat must go out!' And he was gone.

Smith went to the end of the platform again, and from there up the line to find the locomotive foreman, James Roberts. But Roberts had received word from Somerville in the north box, and was already running to it. Once there he tested the signals, and was still desperately testing them when Smith arrived.

'We must go out along the bridge,' said Smith.

'The signals do not work, Mr Smith!'

'The wires are down. The bridge is down. We must go out along the bridge for no one knows what has happened.'

They went out together, moving quickly at first along the bend through the bowstring girder, and the wind was not too strong and Smith had no fear. But once they reached the end of the bend the wind was like a falling wall of wool, pressing them down to their knees, to their bellies. Smith could see nothing, not Roberts, not the bridge ahead of him, not the shore behind, and now he was afraid. He called out.

'Roberts, I can go no farther! I'm too giddy.'

Roberts, crawling ahead, had not heard, so Smith lay on the flooring, holding it with his hands until he found the strength to drag himself back to the signal cabin.

But Roberts went on, pulling himself forward by his hands, pushing with his legs, belly close to the planks, yard by yard for over half a mile, and seeing nothing above or about him. Sometimes he lay still and got back his breath and his courage. He hated the snatches of moonlight for they showed him the heavy anger of the river below. Yet he hated the darkness too, for he could see nothing in it and felt only the terrible vibration of the bridge.

He had been a seaman in his youth and he reminded himself of this when he wanted to turn and go back. He crawled on until, in another interval of moonlight, he saw that there was suddenly nothing left of the bridge for him to crawl upon. Ahead of him stretched a great gap, and below it twelve great tufts of white spray where the river snarled at the broken piers. In the distance was a single red light, and he hoped, with little conviction, that this was the train and that it had been stopped before it reached the gap.

The water-pipe was twisted in the air above him, gushing. The wind drove the spray of it down on him now and then. It was cold and he shivered under it. He lay there for some minutes, waiting for the fragments of moonlight, and with each of them he tried to see and to remember. The railway lines sagged away a foot from his face, curling downward to the river like fern fronds. In the darkness, when the moon passed, he felt with his hands, touching splintered wood and jagged iron.

At last he turned on the pivot of his belly and crawled back, and never knew how long the journey took him.

When he reached Somerville's signal-box there was a great crowd below it, calling up and demanding to know what had happened. Roberts saw the faces upturned, like a pebbled beach left white by the wash of a retreating wave. There were angry men there, who were angry without knowing why, the way men will be angry when they suspect something is being kept from them. There were women and children too, and some of the children were crying in their instinctive awareness of disaster.

Roberts shook his head at them, and at Somerville who was no more frightened by the crowd than by the storm, and he walked wearily back to the station and reported to Smith.

Coming out of his church at about eight o'clock Harbourmaster William Robertson was surrounded by a crowd that shouted 'The bridge is doon!' He hurried to his office and there was Lawson, angry in his exhaustion, declaring that he and other gentlemen had seen the fall of the bridge (which was not strictly accurate, but how else could he refer to those flashes of light?). A boat should go out, he said, a boat *must* go out.

Robertson was confused by the noise, by the lack of information. He called for someone to fetch the Provost quickly, and then he ran up the steps to his observatory, with Lawson behind him, still shouting for a boat.

There were two telescopes in the observatory, one pointing down the estuary, the other up it. Robertson closed the door and opened the window, and he turned one of the glasses towards the bridge. He focused it first on the Wormit bank, and waited for the moonlight that came suddenly in gentle splendour. Robertson followed the line of the girders northwards until the foremast of the *Mars* broke into view. He moved the glass beyond this to where the High Girders should have been seen. He cried out to Lawson 'There is no bridge now!'

He swung the glass to the northern bank and began to move it southward. He stopped suddenly and he said again 'There is no bridge, Mr Lawson. The bridge is gone!'

His distress was great. He ran down from the observatory into the dockyard, hammering on doors in the darkness, his shoulders and elbows forcing aside the crowd. He saw a face he knew, and caught the man's arms, sending him away to get his night-glasses, and he waited impatiently until they came.

He went to the office of the superintendent of the Tay ferries, thinking that he could see the bridge from there, but he could not. So he ran to the Esplanade, with the crowd running behind him, and there he focused his night-glasses and 'the thing was plain, we could see all the stumps standing'.

John Malloch, night reporter on duty in the *Advertiser*'s office, was trying, as night reporters do everywhere, to rest his mind, his feet, and his back at the same time. He was succeeding when Mr Clark came in, and stood there sucking in the smoky air until at last he said. 'There has been a great accident to the bridge. The girders are down and a train too.'

Malloch paused only to warn the composing-room to expect changes, and that these would be made on the main news page, and then he ran all the way to the station. He found Smith waving his hands hopelessly at a dangerously restless crowd that filled South Union Street from wall to wall, sighing and keening to itself. Malloch fought his way through it, and strongly advised Smith to close the doors and to say nothing. He said that there must be relatives in the crowd and there could easily be panic.

At that moment Provost Brownlee's carriage came clopping through the dying rain to the station, the good man's face staring anxiously over the dropped window at the great mass of people. Smith and Malloch went up to him and whispered in his ear that all communication with the south bank was cut. Provost Brownlee knew then that it was true after all, the bridge was down.

He went on to the harbour with Smith, and with the locomotive foreman Roberts, who, sitting in the carriage, told the Provost of the terrible things he had seen out there on the bridge. When they arrived at the docks they found Harbourmaster Robertson, his face red with exasperation, swearing that because it was now low water all the steamers were aground, or had no steam up. They waited impatiently on the slip for the arrival of the Newport ferry, which came up to the pier with agonizing caution because of the low water. It was now almost ten o'clock, more than two hours since the High Girders had fallen.

While the crowd waited, Post-master Gibb came down from

the town, and he took the Provost by the lapel and drew him aside. He had just received a telegram, he said, from the Post-mistress at Broughty Ferry. Mailbags had been washed up on the foreshore there. What did it mean?

'The bridge is down, Mr Gibb,' said the Provost sadly, 'and the train too, I fear.'

The ferry-boat *Dundee* was made fast, and Captain Methven came ashore into the crowd, and the Provost took his hand. 'The bridge is down, Captain. Will you go up? Will you take your steamer up to the bridge?'

'I will do that, Provost. I will do that at once.'

At the station the crowd had become ugly. A woman's voice, shrill, high, in skirling Scots, kept calling 'Wha's ma bairn?' Behind the locked doors the station staff, who knew little of what happened but feared a great deal, waited anxiously. The crowd throbbed backwards and forwards, and in the centre of it men and women began to fight amongst themselves in panic. The glass of the main door cracked and burst inward. From behind it the railwaymen saw a man waving a bloody hand and shouting incoherently until a swirl of the crowd swept him away.

Suddenly the fringes of the mob began to ebb away as a cry went up that there was news at the telegraph office belonging to the Caledonian Railway on Dock Street. There too the doors were locked, and the staff waiting in fright behind them. Out-side waited Mr George Scrymgeour, a gentleman who, on his way home from church, had been abruptly recruited by the Telegraph Superintendent with the plea that he pacify the crowd. Mr Scrymgeour did his best, although he was handi-capped by the fact that he could scarcely believe the bridge was indeed fallen. He shouted bravely that there was no need for alarm, that it was probably a terrible mistake.

Alarm, however, was burning across the city. Light after light spurted suddenly in the windows as people flung back their curtains and started out across the river. Across the water, in Tayport, Newport and Wormit, lights also lit the windows until the whole of Tayside sparkled with their unusual glitter.

Into Dundee from Broughty Ferry to the east there came an almost unbroken chain of galloping carriages, with men standing upright in them, shouting of the strange wreckage that was being washed up along the flats at Lady Bank.

At 10.30 the ferry-boat *Dundee* left for the bridge. Aboard her were Provost Brownlee, Station-master Smith, James Roberts, the Harbour-master, other officers and crews of the ferry service, some gentlemen, and a doctor who took with him 'some medical comforts.'

It was not easy to get the *Dundee* up to the bridge. There was a strong ebb-tide and Captain Methven had to take her well down-river in a wide loop to avoid the sandbanks on the north shore. The crowd along the Esplanade, ten deep now and silent, watched the lights of the little ferry as she fought her way up to the bridge.

It was a few minutes past eleven when Captain Methven anchored her about 200 yards east of the High Girders. Tidal waves were running high and breaking over the *Dundee*'s bows, but the gentlemen pushed forward, wiping the water from their faces and staring up to the sky.

They saw twelve black stumps in the water where the river leaped and played white-headed. And above the stumps there was nothing. Some of the gentlemen wept.

'Please, please!' called Provost Brownlee. 'Pray keep silence. There may be someone calling from the piers.'

They kept silence and they listened, but they heard no call.

Captain Methven asked for a volunteer crew to man the lifeboat. Some of the gentlemen immediately volunteered and were politely rejected. It was too angry a night for amateur seamen. The crew finally picked was headed by Captain Edwards, a ferry-boat commander, and consisted of Harbour-master Robertson, Seamen Eadie and Smith, and Rigger Scott.

They pulled away to the centre of the bridge, pulled hard against the ebb-tide tug, and when they got there Edwards grasped one of the piers and held the boat stationary for a few seconds before his hold was torn away. He ordered the boat round to the north where they took shelter in the lee of the first of the High Girders' piers. The looked up and saw the rails hanging over, the pipe-water laying a great veil over them.

Then away south again, on the side of the bridge this time, because they were frightened to row down the east side lest in that unreliable light they foul the fallen girders. They picked up pieces of planking, and each time a fresh piece was sighted one of the seamen shouted '*Tha's a buidy*!', but it was always a balk of wood.

At twenty-five minutes to midnight they returned to the *Dundee*. Her passengers were hanging over the side calling and asking if a rescue had been made. The boatmen shook their heads and were hauled inboard. Methven turned the ferry back to Dundee.

'We must go out again in the morning!' cried Provost Brownlee, 'and with divers too!'

They went back to the harbour. No more could be done that night, yet few people in the city went to bed. The lights remained on, the curtains drawn back, and men still stood at their windows staring at the river, as if they expected some generous miracle in which the bridge would re-erect itself and the train would steam safely into Tay Bridge Station after all. Or they talked among themselves in hushed voices, and quietened children who were too excited or too frightened to sleep while the world fell down outside their bedroom windows.

The police cordon on the harbour and at the station was increased, and the anger of the waiting crowd died away into grief.

James Smith got word through to Edinburgh by the Caledonian wire. It reached John Stirling, who at once ordered a special train to take him to Dundee as soon as it could be got ready. He sent a telegram to Sir Thomas Bouch, inviting him to come as well.

Bouch was in bed when the telegram came, and he read it as he sat alone in his dressing-gown, and because he was alone nobody knew what expression passed across his face, or what terrible emotions passed through his mind. He called a servant and sent a reply to Stirling. He would come to Dundee at once.

Another man used the Caledonian's wire out of Dundee that night – John Malloch, newspaperman. His duty to his own newspaper was ended for the moment. In the composing-rooms of all the Dundee daily papers the compositors, with some sleep still pricking their eyes, were setting up the single-column, six-deck headlines of disaster.

## TERRIFIC HURRICANE

### APPALLING CATASTROPHE AT DUNDEE

## TAY BRIDGE DOWN

### PASSENGER TRAIN HURLED INTO RIVER

Supposed loss of 200 lives

*Great Excitement*

In the Caledonian's office John Malloch began to send his linage over the wire, via Perth, to the London press. He wrote quickly on a pad of telegraph forms.

Monday 1.30 a.m. The scene at the Tay Bridge Station tonight is simply appalling. Many thousands of persons are congregated around the building, and strong men and women are wringing their hands in despair ...

# IV

*'Their friends and relations they ran to the station
The fate of some loved one all eager to know'*

ALL night the crowds waited, outside Tay Bridge Station, at the
Harbour, or along the Esplanade. They waited for daylight. Daylight would show them the bridge. And while they waited they
fed themselves with rumour. There had been 300 people aboard
the train. There had been nobody aboard but the Company's
servants. The train had not even been on the bridge, it was still
at St Fort. The shore between Wormit and Tayport was strewn
with bodies. There were wee bairns floating off Lady Bank with
only their poor faces above water. A man ... what man? ... a
man living along Magdalen Green ... had heard a woman weeping out on the bridge, and the sound of her weeping had gone on
for an hour or more. The High Girders had been destroyed by a
bomb, by lightning, by an earth tremor. The workmen who
built the bridge had frequently been drunk. Thomas Bouch was
a charlatan who had never built a bridge before this.

This man, or that woman, calling violently from out the dark
belly of the crowd, declared his or her conviction that the
bridge had been against God's will, and in His wrath had He
destroyed it.

Yet nobody knew anything, nobody knew more than the Harbour officials, and that was little enough. The High Girders were
down, and with them a train.

The sun rose at 8.47 a.m. on Monday, 29 December 1879, with
the tide on the ebb. Before this there had been half an hour of
tween-light in which the broken bridge took shape with horrible
reluctance, first in thin outlines and then in firmer form until in
the glistening opal light, it was there for all to see. The people
along Tayside, from Broughty Ferry to Cartagena Bank, stared

in silence at the twelve bare stumps which were 'like columns of some majestic ruin of antiquity'.

The river ran smoothly, cream-coloured, and scarcely ruffled enough to snarl white at the foot of the piers.

Before breakfast Mr Gibb, the Postmaster, hurried through the streets to the Provost's house with a telegram. It was from Sir Henry Ponsonby. *Can you give me any particulars of the appalling calamity reported to have taken place? The Queen is inexpressibly shocked and feels most deeply for those who have lost friends and relatives in this terrible accident.*

In his dressing-gown, unshaven, his eyes dry from a night without sleep, Provost Brownlee wrote his reply, telling Sir Henry all that he knew, all that he believed. He followed the official statement made by the North British Railway, that 'it deeply regretted to say that there were nearly 300 passengers, beside the Company's servants, in the train'.

This was the belief that Monday morning, that the 5.20 from Burntisland had been carrying three hundred passengers. And it is true that on any other day of the week it would have been so. Yet nobody seems to have realized or remembered that on Sundays the train never carried more than a third of this number. So, until Station-agent Robert Morris came over the Tay from St Fort, the city grieved its three hundred dead.

In his pocket Morris carried the fifty-seven tickets which he and his staff had collected. He remembered the two season ticket holders, and he remembered that ten or eleven passengers had retained their tickets. The sum was simple and quickly done. Provost Brownlee announced the loss of seventy-five men, women and children. But who were they? What were their names? Where had they lived? Wearily, the Provost asked Station-master Smith to make discreet inquiries among the waiting crowds.

The news went across Britain by the electric telegraph. In their later editions that Monday all daily newspapers replaced their lead stories. News of the storming of Shepur, of the struggle about Kabul, of the anxiety felt for General Roberts' forces in Afganistan, gave way before The Tay Bridge Disaster.

Its impact on the British public was greater than the emotional shock normally struck by a terrible catastrophe. Down into the Tay with the High Girders had gone Britain's pride in her talent and industry, and it was this pride that made many people at first reluctant to believe that the bridge had really fallen. When they did believe they were angry at the betrayal. The anger lingered on, and was so powerful that it has been held partly responsible for the defeat of Lord Beaconsfield's government in the general election three months later.

Yet it must be admitted that not everybody felt the shock or the betrayal. From the Caledonian Railway's heartland the *Glasgow Herald* said: 'It is easy to be wise after the event, but it must not be forgotten that the melancholy event of last night has been more than once fore-shadowed by the opponents of this great engineering scheme.'

Patrick Matthew's ghost had arisen and spoken.

In Dundee, however, men and women were too close to the disaster for philosophic reflection. During Monday morning the crowds increased, particularly outside the station. There were mostly relatives – wives, parents, children – who came for news and could be given no news, and certainly no comfort. And there were idlers who came, as they come everywhere, to be thrilled by the naked grief of others. With each successive rumour that a body had been recovered from the Tay the crowd surged silently against the doors of the station.

Along the Esplanade many gentlemen stood in their carriages with field-glasses to their eyes, describing the view for the benefit of those on the roadway. Out from Dundee harbour flowed a little armada of small steamers, wherries, tugs, fishing-boats, yachts, that weaved in and out of the broken piers, with passengers hanging over their sides and staring into the water. The river, a satiated animal, betrayed nothing, revealed nothing, and tolerated this curiosity until it tired of it. It suddenly drew a mist about the bridge, and then drove away the boats with a series of angry squalls. At midday the river was empty, and the sun came out, smiling serenely.

At first-light, when day had been no more than a bar of dull silver across the mouth of the firth, the steam-launch *Fairweather* had nosed in and out of the piers. The harbour diver, Edward Simpson, was aboard her, and so was Harbour-master Robertson, and James Yeaman, M.P. She also carried a number of workmen equipped with iron hooks, ropes, grappling irons. Made fast to her side was a crane barge, and on this was the diving apparatus.

In the dusk of dawn she passed a long-boat from the *Mars* with Captain Scott aboard. He hailed and he said that he had been out for an hour or more with sounding leads and long poles, trying to find the train. It was his opinion, coming across the thin light and leaden water, that the train lay near the south end of the bridge where a portion of girder could be seen above water. The tide was ebbing fast, and as the long-boat bobbed away Captain Scott's voice could be heard calling a warning to beware of sunken debris.

Ashore, a train had come in from Perth. Sir Thomas Bouch, wrapped in a heavy ulster, gripping his son's elbow firmly and striding unhesitatingly through the silent crowd, went on to find Provost Brownlee and the Harbour-master. He was told that Robertson was out on the river, and he listened without comment to all that was known about the fall of his bridge. He was treated politely, but without warmth. To everybody he turned the blank, ungiving expression of his face. Only the fact that he had brought his son with him revealed his inner need for comfort. This son was the boy, now a man, who had stood by Bouch's side at Wormit nine years before.

Bouch said that he would like to visit the bridge as soon as possible. He was told that the steamer *Forfarshire* was going out that morning and that the master would be glad to take him. Bouch nodded, sat down in the harbour offices, and appears to have spoken to no one unless first addressed. His son stood with him.

Out on the Tay, Diver Simpson had found little. The *Fairweather* had moved northward along the broken piers of the High Girders, taking soundings, and when the lead showed six and a half feet only the steamer halted. Simpson, helmet bolted on, went slowly over the side of the barge by the seventh pier from the south side. The water was dark and murky, thick with disturbed mud and sand, and he could see little or nothing. Yet this darkness hid a train and perhaps the bodies of seventy-five people.

But Simpson found a girder, that he could not miss for one end of it projected above the river. He came up. They took the helmet from his head and gave him water. He was sweating. He shook his head. 'It's too muddy. I can see nothing.'

Grappling irons were traced over the girder below water, and they came up with nothing but a tangle of telegraph wires. Robertson took the *Fairweather* from pier to pier. The masonry bases seemed undamaged, and through the water now the men on the steamer could see the bars of some of the columns. The cast-iron struts moved and waved like weeds below the passage of the swift water.

At 10 a.m. the *Forfarshire* left Dundee Harbour for the bridge, her decks crowded with passengers including the Provost, James Cox, Dugald Drummond and Sir Thomas Bouch. Bouch stood forward, lonely in his ulster, and no one cared to speak with him because his emotions were so plain in the hunch of his shoulders. Now and then he turned his head to answer a question or receive a word of comfort from his son, but most of the time he looked upriver to the bridge that had been his dream for twenty years.

The *Forfarshire* passed up and down the bridge, and it remained there when the *Fairweather* went back. It remained there, turning and returning, leaving the black weave of its smoke in the air, until it too went back to Dundee with nothing proved and little discovered.

'There is another diver,' said Harbour-master Robertson diffidently. 'A good man at Broughty Ferry. Peter Harley. He is accustomed to deep sea work.'

Bouch spoke suddenly. 'I shall be obliged if you will telegraph this man, Captain Robertson, and ask him if he will come at once.'

All morning Robertson was there on the docks, moving from

one gentleman to another with scraps of information, some of it inconsequential, some of it of importance, as if he wanted them to know everything, as if he wanted them to know that he was doing everything. The level of ebb-tide that night, he said, had been three and a half feet lower than usual. It showed, he said, the power of the hurricane, as if this had not already been proved by the fall of the bridge.

Smith and Sons, cabinet-makers and undertakers of Dundee, received word from Provost Brownlee. One of the largest re-freshment-rooms at Tay Bridge Station, he said, was being cleared for the reception of the dead. The floor of this room was being laid with wagon covers. The Provost would be obliged if Mr Smith would take charge of the matter and 'prepare shells for the bodies'.

The first black-horse-drawn carriage that clattered to the station produced an upheaval among the crowd like the rippling fold of a shaken sheet. Men and women cried out and moved in closer, and the long-tailed horses stepped sideways in alarm and beat on the cobbles with their hooves. The Station-master, his nerve recovered now, and in command of himself, came out and held up his hands for silence. There was no news, he said, there was no news of the dead.

About three in the afternoon a squall of rain came up from the Ochils, born on a strong, beating wind. The sky darkened again over the whole estuary, and the rain turned the black slates to pewter, and stippled the surface of the river with hail. It was dark, very dark by four o'clock, and the Esplanade was at last deserted. The last carriage, its oil lamp flickering, was gone.

Only outside the Station was there a crowd still, a small one and mostly relatives. Among them were three young women, the sisters Cheape from Lochee, whose mother had been aboard the train. They stood together and shook their heads silently when the church women who were in attendance offered them tea or soup.

Just before sunset the *Fairweather* had gone out again with a diver called Fox aboard. But he looked at the rising wind and he looked at the water, and he shook his head. He would not go down. He had heard that Peter Harley was coming from Broughty Ferry, and he seemed resentful. Let Harley go down, then. He would not.

The North British Railway issued another statement from Edinburgh. All through-traffic to the north was discontinued. There would be no trains to Aberdeen until further notice. Traffic, if any, would be routed through Perth.

Correspondents and artists from the English press were arriving in Dundee, or were on their way there. They filled the rooms of the Royal Hotel and waited in its lobby for their fellow-guest Sir Thomas Bouch. At the harbour they bid for the exclusive services of the boatmen. They made quick friends with harbour and railway officials, and they bullied Mr Gibb, the Postmaster, into organizing an efficient telegraph service. The world's Press was asking its London representatives for the fullest details.

In the night-dark, with hail rattling on the windows behind him, Station-master Smith again told the waiting relatives (whom he had now admitted to a third-class waiting-room) that there was no body yet recovered.

But there was.

Just before sunset, off Greenside Scalp to the north-east of Newport, and three miles from the bridge, a mussel-dredger had seen a dark shape drifting between two sand-banks. He rowed over to it and there was the body of a woman dressed in black. Her white face turned to the sky, the black ribbon of her poke-bonnet was still tied beneath her chin. Her black skirts floated wide and her feet were together.

The mussel-dredger reached for her with a hook, and the body turned over at his touch and bobbed away, and it was only with some difficulty that he got it aboard.

It was taken to Dundee and to the station. There it was laid on a wagon sheet in the refreshment-room. There was nothing in the pockets to identify it, nothing but a railway ticket to Broughty Ferry. The three sisters Cheape, hearing that the body of a middle-aged woman had been recovered, burst screaming into the room and fell on their knees beside it.

Then they stood up. They shook their heads and wept. This, they said, was not their mother  It was not. It was, although nobody knew it yet, Ann Cruickshank, housemaid to Lady Baxter of Kilmaron. An ordinary woman who had ended an uneventful life by being the first body to be recovered from the Tay Bridge disaster.

# V

*'In this gay and festive season
We must deplore the loss of life'*

MRS UPTON, of Union Street, Dundee, had been weeping since Sunday night, but on Tuesday morning she dried her eyes and ran out of her house, calling and laughing and shouting to her neighbours. All night she had waited at the station for the body of her daughter Alice, a girl of sixteen who had been aboard the train, or so Mrs Upton believed.

But in the early hours of Tuesday, as she went home for breakfast, she met one of Mr Gibbs' messengers who was carrying a telegram from Alice, in which the girl asked her mother's forgiveness for having stayed overnight at Edinburgh on Sunday. When Mrs Upton had called her neighbours from their doors she went down on her knees and prayed.

There was, however, no such good news for the four brothers of Robert Watson. They stood in the third-class waiting-room at the station, and the blind brother held himself erect with his face lifted in an expression of patient supplication. Station-master Smith moved softly about the relatives and he whispered that the *Fairweather* was out on the river again, searching for bodies.

The steamer had gone out early. From the foreshore she could be seeing lying off the broken stumps, her head pointed into the current, a thread of black smoke drawn taut from her stack to her after-mast. Close by was the barge from which the divers were working, and on this barge was Peter Harley, a great man with a blunt face and a noble head. He was angrily asking why nobody had warned him to bring his gear.

Diver Fox was 19 feet below the surface, moving slowly through the dark water, afraid for his suit and his airline in the muddy whirls that hid the knife-edges of the broken iron. He saw nothing, and he felt nothing but the debris.

Henry Noble, Inspector of the bridge, was aboard the *Fair-weather* and much worried. At mid-morning his name was called from the broken end of the bridge on the north side. He went forward and looked up to the little group of workmen who were holding tight to the gas-pipe and bending down over the gap. He answered their hail, and waved his hat so that they might pick him out from the crowd on the steamer's deck. They shouted that Major Marindin, Inspector for the Board of Trade, was at Dundee docks and wished to come out to the bridge.

Noble answered irritably. He said that if he put the *Fair-weather* in now he would lose the ebb-tide, and diving would become impossible once it turned to flood. But he was told that the Major insisted, and the *Fairweather* went back to Dundee.

Marindin's name was acting like a key in a well-oiled lock. Late on Monday it had been announced that a Board of Trade Inquiry into the disaster would open in Dundee that week, and that all facilities were to be given to its officers. Marindin was such an officer, and so was Major-General Hutchinson, who had come up to Dundee that morning (presumably with a copy of his report in his luggage).

The *Fairweather* took both gentlemen aboard and set out again for the bridge. With them went Bouch and Colonel Yolland, M.P. Old Dugald Drummond was aboard too, swearing that if only divers looked they would find the engine-driver on the foot-plate.

The streets of Dundee were full. It was a market day and there were many people from the inland towns and villages of Forfar. They stood on the corners and in the shops and they talked of the bridge. They made visits of frank curiosity to the station to see the waiting relatives, and they listened to the rumours, embroidering them extravagantly before retelling them.

Fox and Simpson dived again from the barge that afternoon. Fox came up after a few minutes, but Simpson was below water for nearly half an hour, and when he was pulled inboard his face was grey and his lips were blue, and it was a long time before he could talk. He said that he had walked 40 feet along the inside of the High Girders and he had seen nothing but the iron.

Now Fox went down from the steamer, and when he came up again after seven minutes there was a great shout from the deck. His hand broke the flurry of yellow water first, and he waved it slowly. They took his helmet off. 'We've got something now,' he said, 'I've found a coach!'

He told them to haul on his line which he had made fast to something below, but Harbour-master Robertson, afraid that the line would break, ordered Fox below again. He came up with a piece of blue waxcloth, and on it were the letters 'NBR' in a diamond scroll. He had also some horsehair and cloth from the lining of the first-class coach. He said that he had found the coach close to the iron straps which laced the girders together on the top.

He could say nothing more for some minutes, so they let him rest, and then he went on to say he had entered the coach by the window, the top of which was broken.

'Did you find a body?' he was asked.

'I put my hand on what I thought was a corpse. I pulled and it came away, but it was part of the upholstery.'

Where was the coach? He thought that it was inside the fourth or the fifth of the fallen girders, about forty feet east of the pier-bases.

The gentlemen were suddenly silent, looking at the diver as he sat there in his wet suit, his tired face still above the great iron ring of his collar. Some of them shivered. It was now dark and a strong ebb-tide was running. The lights of the *Fairweather* were draining blood on the black water, and a wind was rising.

They returned to Dundee, and they said that they had found the train.

But the people cared little about this discovery, or the waxcloth and horse-hair, or Diver Fox's uneasy recollections of the silent ruin beneath the river. They wanted to know why no bodies had been discovered.

All day along the foreshore at Broughty Ferry the Tay had been throwing up debris – hats, shoes, shawls, papers, bags, cushions, cloaks – a dreadful flotsam that was reverently collected and put on the train for Dundee. There it was placed on display in the mortuary that had once been a refreshment-room. The relatives of the missing filed past it silently, staring at each article, searching for something familiar that would tell them what they feared to know.

John Malloch, of the *Advertiser*, leant against the wall with his pencil and his notebook, and when an article was recognized, that is when a woman fainted or a child screamed, he came forward gently to put his soft, understanding question.

The gas light shone yellow on the little piles of clothing. There was Guard David Johnston's cap, and the basket containing his flags neatly rolled. They were recognized by his young wife, who came to the station with a boy of five at her skirt and a baby of nine weeks wrapped in a shawl. She did not faint. She wept as she told Malloch that her husband had not been on duty with the train, but had been travelling to Dundee to work on the first train south on Monday morning.

There was also Driver Mitchell's cap, and the cap of his stoker Marshall. There was a woman's handbag containing a Bible, a pair of spectacles, a purse, a bunch of keys, and a neat package of temperance pledge cards issued by the Catholic Association for the Suppression of Drunkenness.

There was a gentleman's vest and a dress shirt rolled in a handkerchief. There was a box containing a dozen table-knives and table-forks with mother of pearl handles.

There were two chemises and two pairs of handkerchiefs also wrapped in a handkerchief. There was an Indian sewn petticoat with a card attached to it. It said *With D. W. Ferrier's compliments*. There was Jessie Bain's muff, in the pocket of which was the love-letter from her sweetheart. There were two packets of tea, and there was an empty hamper which, if the invoice still pinned to it was correct, had contained 30 Leicestershire pies when it left Burntisland.

All these things, and many more, were spaced out on wagon-cloths. Against the opposite wall Ann Cruickshank lay waiting for company, and for someone to give her a name.

Shortly before nine o'clock in the evening somebody did so. A woman walked swiftly into the room and looked down as the face was uncovered, and Ann Cruickshank was no longer 'an unidentified body of a matron aged about sixty years'.

With darkness little parties of men, volunteers but led by police-constables, began to patrol the river-banks from the bridge to Broughty Ferry and Tayport. They kept close to the water's edge, looking for more wreckage, looking for more bodies. The light of their torches and their lanterns could be seen from Dundee, blots of moving colour against the darkness.

At Broughty Ferry the excise officers took charge of the luggage that was still being washed up. In Dundee the harassed officials of the North British Railway decided that on the morrow the passenger ferry service would be reopened from Broughty Ferry to Tayport. The railway connection to the south would operate as it had always done until eighteen months ago. It was as if the bridge never existed.

The first outside expression of grief and sympathy (apart from Her Gracious Majesty's) arrived in Dundee. It came from a group of Liberals in Hanley, Staffordshire, who had been celebrating the seventieth birthday of William Ewart Gladstone when news of the disaster reached them.

Here and there throughout Scotland men and women discovered that but for the Grace of God, or the accident of history, they too might have been aboard the train.

'... Mr and Mrs Brown, who had been in Edinburgh from Dundee on a wedding tour, were to have returned home on Sunday afternoon. They were, however, pressed at a small party to remain and at the last moment, chiefly on account of the boisterous weather, they were reluctantly persuaded to postpone the day of their return ...'

'... Another gentleman, who intended to join the train at Abbeyhill, was saved by the stratagem of his wife, who adopted means to keep him at home ...'

One of the last articles to be found on the sand-banks that

Tuesday night was 'a small fancy hand-basket such as young ladies carry'. It was never claimed.

The Great McGonagall was inspired by the disaster. He began his poem on Monday and he had finished it before dusk on Tuesday. There were 59 lines, of which the last nine read

> Oh! ill-fated Bridge of the Silv'ry Tay,
> I must now conclude my lay
> By telling the world fearlessly without the least dismay
> That yur central girders would not have given way,
> At least many sensible men do say,
> Had they been supported on each side with buttresses,
> At least many sensible men confesses,
> For the stronger we our houses do build,
> The less chance we have of being killed.

On Wednesday morning Mr F. W. Pope Cox, of the Telephone Company, Ltd, offered the North British Railway the use of a set of Bell's telephones for communicating between shore and diving barges. The offer was found to be impracticable, but it indicated what *The Times* was describing as 'the impatience felt by the public at the barrenness of the diving operations'.

The public did not care what scraps of clothing or pieces of planking were taken from the river. For two nights it had gone to bed, or not gone to bed according to the state of its imagination, with the knowledge that there were many bodies below the surface of the river, and no one yet knew where. This was both blasphemous and obscene. The sight of the group of relatives still waiting for news at the station was no longer a curiosity, but something to be avoided because of the pain it gave. There was anger at the river for taking the dead, and there was stronger anger against the authorities for not recovering them speedily. In a deeply religious Scotland that believed in paying Death its full measure of ceremony and ritual, the disaster could never be ended so long as one body remained hidden below the water.

The authorities were as anxious as the public to recover the bodies, but with the Board of Trade Inquiry about to take place they were even more anxious to determine the position and nature of the fallen girders. Mr Noble's steam launch, which he had used for his regular inspections during the time the bridge was in use, went out at eight a.m., just before sunrise on Wednesday. It was a small craft and of light draught. Diver Simpson was aboard.

There were dark, heavy clouds to the west as the sun rose, but here and there were ragged tears through which the sun dropped down on the snow-topped Highlands in slanting columns of gold. The launch was moored a few yards to the south of the fifth pier of the High Girders, and Simpson went over the side, standing on the ladder while his helmet was screwed on.

The deck of the launch was crowded with gentlemen who had turned up their collars against the wind. There was General Hutchinson, Major Marindin, and old Dugald Drummond, still convinced that his driver would be found on the footplate of No. 224. There were some English journalists, and an artist from the *Illustrated London News* who crouched on his buttocks up against a bulkhead, at work with pencil and paper.

At 9.20 a.m., with an hour yet to low tide, Simpson went below and remained below for a quarter of an hour. He came up and said that he had found four pieces of a carriage but no bodies. He went down again, this time on the north side of the launch, and the artist moved over the better to catch the dramatic effect of the helmet disappearing below the water. On board the launch there was silence as all watched the little thread of bubbles that marked Simpson's slow movements below. He came up shortly, his helmet bouncing on the water, and he tapped rapidly on his face glass. They unscrewed it.

*'I've found the engine!'*

It was, he said, lying on its side in the fifth span of the High Girders, funnel pointing east, its head towards the north. He had seen the tender too. Sand was rapidly silting over both.

Dugald Drummond pushed forward. 'Look!' he said, and he took Simpson's arm. He called for a pencil and he began to draw on the deck. 'There!' he said, and he stabbed a thumb at the

guiding lever in the cabin of the engine he had drawn, 'There!
You'll find the driver there.'

Simpson went down again, and was below for ten minutes
before he came up. He was holding the driver's lamp. Dugald
Drummond leant over the ship's side, his hand on Simpson's
shoulder, and he could scarcely wait for the face-piece to be
unscrewed. He shouted 'Did ye find him?'

Simpson sucked in the air and then shook his head. He had
found no bodies. Dugald Drummond was shocked.

Later that morning Fox, diver for the Harbour Trustees, went
down from the crane barge, and Peter Harley went down from
another barge. They moved in sluggish water, in silted sand and
in mud, and they found a lamp or two but nothing more. Again,
in the afternoon, while Brownlee, Drummond and Robertson
fretted on deck, the divers went down again. They were beginning to complain of the cold now, but still they went below
when ordered, coming up at last into the red glimmer of lanterns. It was late and the search was abandoned for another
night.

Harbour-master Robertson had a theory. He said that when
the carriages crashed into the water compressed air blew off the
roof, and the 'doomed occupants' were shot out into the river
like peas from a snapped pod. It sounded a feasible explanation
to all except Dugald Drummond, who could not believe that
there was anything that could shake a driver from his footplate.

One thing was certain. No bodies were likely to be found near
the bridge now, and Provost Brownlee said that he would have
search parties walking the sand flats at low tide, night and day.
That night their torches once more pricked the darkness.

Once identified, Ann Cruickshank's body had been taken
away from the refreshment-room by the dark gentlemen from
Smith & Sons. A large crowd followed the hearse up the street to
the undertakers' rooms, and waited outside without quite knowing why. The public was uneasy. The surface of its emotions
itched at the thought of so many bodies out there in the river.

Captain Lindsay Brine, of H.M.S. *Lord Warden*, Superintendent of Coastguards for the north-east of Scotland, had

been aboard the *Fairweather* in the afternoon, and when he came ashore there was a telegram awaiting him from the Admiralty. He was instructed to give every help in the search for bodies, and to make full use of the diving suits aboard the *Lord Warden*.

Word came from the Duke of Buccleuch. He had a diving suit, he said, an admission that surprised many people who wondered what on earth he needed it for. He said that he was dispatching it to Dundee at once.

Early on Wednesday stationers in the city had filled their windows with tastefully printed memorial cards, heavily bordered with black and bearing verses of sympathy and condolence. At lamp-light ballad-mongers hoarsely cried the streets

> 'In this gay and festive season
> We must deplore the loss of life!'

Ashore Fox and Harley said little of their experiences below water by the bridge, and seemed resentful when questioned by the Press. But Simpson found his voice and exercised it fully. 'It's a relief,' he said, or he was reported as saying once his Scots was filtered into English, 'to get off that heavy, air-tight helmet. But it's an even greater relief to be rid of the breast-plate and the leads, each of which weighs 28 lb. and are attached to my back and chest. In addition to those weights I carry 14 lb. of lead plate on the bottom of my sea-boots.'

He agreed that more divers were needed. They came, late on Wednesday night, from the gunboats *Firm* and *Netley* of Captain Brine's command.

At the Royal Hotel the gentlemen who had hurried north to conduct the Board of Trade Inquiry decided that there was nothing as yet into which they could inquire with any profit. They would leave for the south in the morning, but they would return at the week-end.

All day more wreckage had beached itself at Broughty Ferry. Bare-legged children, shivering in the bitter December wind, had waded out into the shallows and dragged ashore planks of wood thickly clogged with pitch. They had brought in heavy beams that were once supports of the bridge. They found woodwork from the flooring, with blue-painted iron stanchions still bolted to it. There was a door too, a door from the second-class carriage, and although it must have been wrenched away with great force its window was still unbroken.

There was more known now about the state of the fallen girders and the fallen train. Piers, girders, train lay on the east side of the bridge, and the train was inside the fourth and fifth spans of the High Girders, counting from the Wormit bank, that is. The throttle of the engine was open, and its Westinghouse brake was unapplied. The inference was plain – the train had just entered the High Girders when they fell, and Driver Mitchell had had no warning of disaster.

But had the train brought down the Girders, or had the High Girders brought down the train? That no one was able to say, nor ever would be with any certainty.

Two meetings were held that Wednesday evening.

The Council called the public to the Town Hall. It was a bad night, with a heavy squall on the river and beating rain on the roof slates, but the Hall was filled with silent men and women. Provost Brownlee stood up before them and read the reports of the three days' diving operations. He spoke of many people bereaved, of widows and unhappy orphans. He proposed:

That this meeting of the inhabitants of Dundee desires to express its deepest sympathy with the friends of all those who were suddenly swept into eternity by the stupendous disaster of the Tay Bridge, and that a Committee be appointed to receive subscriptions and to administer the funds that may be subscribed according to the necessities of the case.

The proposal was seconded and unanimously approved.

There was, said Brownlee, £1,980 16s. already donated. This included £500 given by the North British Railway, and another £500 made up of individual subscriptions from the directors of the company.

It also included a banker's cheque for £250. The signature on the cheque was that of Thomas Bouch.

The other meeting was held in Edinburgh. John Stirling was in the chair, and he told his directors what was so far known about the fall of the bridge and of how it lay beneath the River Tay. It was an unproductive meeting and could settle nothing. At the back of each director's mind was the knowledge that the Company's shares had fallen 8½ per cent on Monday and were likely to fall further. The Company had had eighteen months of unprecedented good fortune that now seemed like a dream. Not a few of the men there at that meeting believed that there would be no further insane efforts to bridge the Firth of Tay.

One of them took Stirling's arm when the meeting ended. Surely, he asked, after such a terrible catastrophe the whole futile scheme would be abandoned? Stirling answered without hesitation. He said 'The Tay will again be bridged.'

On the river that night, when the squall died away shortly before ten o'clock, Dundee boatmen took parties of sightseers out to view the bridge by torch-light. And in the composing-room of the *Advertiser* a compositor was setting a letter for the correspondence column. It had been written by a reader who signed himself 'Covenanter'.

According to the theory of probabilities the odds were six to one against the bridge giving way on the Sabbath. But the North British Railway Company has been alike heedless of God's law and man's expostulations . . .

# VI

*'The fall of the bridge is a judgement'*

AFTER its slow beginning, when the paralysis of the disaster held time in suspension, the week moved rapidly towards its close, and the gentlemen of the Board of Trade came back to Dundee to conduct their Inquiry.

On Thursday Captains Adams and Yule, of the whalers *Artic* and *Resolute*, offered the services of their ships and their crews in the search for bodies. Both vessels cruised off the mouth of the firth, and sent away boats to explore the sandbanks. In the bow and stern of each boat stood harpooners with boat-hooks ready.

The North British Railway announced that it would pay a bounty of £5 for every body recovered, and a Mr Tweeney arrived in Dundee seeking Peter Harley. He was a lawyer, and he told the diver that he was acting for the relatives of Mr William Henry Benyon. They were prepared to pay £20 to anyone who recovered the body of the fine art lithographer. It was Mr Tweeney's opinion that Peter Harley was the most likely man to do this.

The *Fairweather* went out whenever it could, high tide or low tide, and always with a great crowd aboard. Bouch went often, still silent or brusque when approached by reporters. There was also the contractor, Edgar Gilkes, and he spoke to the Press. He said: 'I am extremely grieved by the disaster and I'm sorry to find the bridge in this state.' And this did not seem much of an overstatement when it was printed the next day.

Diver Simpson became petulant again. He was, he said, working under extreme difficulties compared with Harley. He did not say so, but perhaps he had heard of Mr Tweeney's offer and resented its inference that Harley was the best diver on the Tay (as indeed he was). Harley, said Simpson, had a long ladder and could reach the river-bed easily, whereas he had a ladder less than seven feet in length. Thus he was forced to make an uncomfortable drop from the end of it to the bed.

All the divers continued to bring up cushions, scraps of upholstery and floor-cloth, planks, boards, and information about the position of the girders and the train. The information was of great value to the directors of the Tay Bridge Undertaking, but it gave no satisfaction at all to the public. The public wanted bodies.

Just why there were none as yet (beyond Miss Cruickshank) was explained by the crews of the fifteen whale-boats that searched the mouth of the firth. The whalers came ashore in the evenings and sat in the dram-shops and sang and talked. They said that a drowned man would not rise to the surface before seven days had elapsed. But for the fact that Ann Cruickshank had drifted into the shallows she too would still be at the bottom of the river.

This made her funeral the more interesting on Thursday. She was mourned by the whole of Dundee. A great crowd followed the hearse from Smith & Sons' establishment to the ferry. Hearse and horses dripped with black crêpe, and there were several ministers in attendance. A band played the cortège mournfully through the cobbled streets and on to the deck of the ferry-boat. There was she carried across the Tay to the Fifeshire bank and away to Kilmaron.

Three more divers came up to Dundee to work on the bridge. A man called Barclay from Shield, another, Gray, from Newcastle, and a naval diver called Tate.

Late on Thursday afternoon, off the Abertay Light and far out in the mouth of the firth where the long sea roll takes and absorbs the water that has travelled down from Ben Lui, one of Captain Adams' whale-boats found a body floating serenely. They rowed for it and fished for it with their hooks. It played a game with them, turning over and over gently at each touch, until at last it sank down with black skirt swirling. And as it went down a beautiful tortoise-shell comb broke free from the dark hair and rose to the surface.

Captain Adams took the comb ashore and left it in the re-freshment-room at Tay Bridge Station, where it was later identified by Jessie Bain's sweetheart.

The Editor of the *Dundee Advertiser* marked another letter for press and sent it down to the composing-room. This was signed 'Observer'.

The Company are not content with the fruit of six days' working but covet and use the seventh. The fall of the bridge is a judgement!

On Friday morning a violent westerly gale sprang up suddenly and hit the *Fairweather* in midstream as she was towing the diving-barge out to the bridge. She carried on against the heavy swell and then lost heart, running for harbour with sleet and hail rattling on her counter. There was no diving that day.

But, although the weather was too bad for the divers, off the flats by Broughty Ferry, Abertay Sands, and Budden Ness scores of small boats searched for bodies. There were now 82 men from the whaling fleets controlled by the Dundee Seal and Whale Fishing Company. A deputation of Broughty Ferry fishermen called on Provost Brownlee and told him that they proposed to go out day and night. The mussel-dredgers sent word that they would do the same.

The Relief Fund had now reached £2,601 17s 6d., and the Misses Wallace of Lochee called several of their friends together and agreed that they should hold a genteel musicale to raise more money.

Station-master James Smith began to receive small photo-graphs of those believed drowned in the Tay, sent in the hope that he would use them to identify the victims. He kept them in his desk, for there was as yet nothing to identify, and the damp patch which the body of Ann Cruickshank had made on the wagon sheet had long since dried.

In Edinburgh, Stirling's firm courage stiffened his fellow directors and they issued a statement.

'The resolution of the directors,' said the *Advertiser*, 'that the bridge shall be rebuilt as soon as possible, has the support of the entire community.' Which was somewhat of an exaggeration since the community had scarcely recovered from the fall of the first bridge.

The directors of the Company also made another decision. All work on the Forth Bridge would cease, and its design would be taken from the hands of Sir Thomas Bouch.

This may have aroused Bouch to talk to the Press. He admitted a reporter to his room at the Royal Hotel, and the reporter went away and perhaps he wrote his story and saw it spiked, or perhaps he merely passed the information by word of mouth to his editor; for the only reference to the interview appeared in the *Advertiser's* lead column.

Sir Thomas Bouch is anxious to show that the circumstances in which the bridge broke down were entirely exceptional. The public, however, will require very strong guarantees for the security of the restored bridge.

And below his hotel window Bouch heard the ballad-mongers calling:

> 'There a crash – an instant's glaring,
>  Unheard shrieks and prayers ablending,
> Hearts a breaking, iron rending,
> One dark plunge – the work is done!'

He rarely left the room except to go to the docks, travelling by carriage, and always in his son's company. Urchins ran after his carriage in the dust of its wheels.

John Walker, General Manager of the North British Railway, a hard man sometimes called 'the Napoleon of British railways', was in charge of the Company's affairs at Dundee. He wrote to the Chief Constables of Fife and Forfarshire, asking them to 'instruct their officers to keep a diligent lookout along the shore'. He further asked that when a body was found the greatest care should be taken of it. He said that there were relatives waiting in Dundee on whom the shock of seeing their dead would be great enough, without having to endure the sight of any mutilation caused by hooks and grapnels.

The relatives, many of whom had come a long distance and had now been waiting for five days, had found residence in the hotels or the little rooming-houses of the city. They were easily recognized in the streets, for they wore heavy mourning clothes and walked swiftly with heads bent. Every morning they went down to Tay Bridge Station and waited there silently. Every day they left with Station-master Smith some scrap of information, the number of a key, the cut of a waistcoat, the position of a birthmark, that would help towards identification. Smith noted all these down in his book and felt himself growing old rapidly.

By Friday evening it was agreed that, as a result of the great quantity of wreckage that had been salvaged from the sand-flats at the mouth of the firth, very little of the carriages as yet undiscovered by the divers could be remaining inside the fallen girders. The heavy tides, the squalls that had beaten spitefully at the river that week, had broken them up and in the night-darkness driven the wood and the leather and the cloth out to sea, like a child guiltily sweeping away the evidence of its sins.

Yet odd things remained that the run of the river should have taken far from the bridge. A child, paddling in muddied boots along the shore below the Esplanade, found a woman's seal-skin hat, bobbing in a back swirl of water. It was taken to Station-master Smith. It was, he noted, 'a good deal torn and damaged,' and none of the waiting relatives recognized it.

There was fine sunshine on Saturday morning, and it was hard for some people to decide whether to go out in a boat and watch the divers at work, or whether to go up to the Sheriff's Court and hear the first day of the Board of Trade Inquiry.

Those who went to the Court were disappointed, for no sooner was it sitting than the Wreck Commissioner, Mr Henry Cadogan Rothery, decided that in view of the fine weather the Court might as well go out on the river and view the scene of the disaster.

The Inquiry was accordingly adjourned until two o'clock that afternoon.

The Court consisted of three men: Mr Rothery, a man of sharp, inquisitive turn of mind and independence of opinion; Colonel William Yolland, R.E., Chief Inspector of Railways for the Board of Trade; and Mr William Henry Barlow, President of the Institute of Civil Engineers They sat in the brown Assize Court, above a flurry of clerks, court reporters, and newspapermen, and they sat there throughout the afternoon until the gas lamps were lit and the yellow light struck darker shadows on their faces. They and the counsels acting for the Board of Trade, the North British Railway Company, asked 597 questions from seven witnesses.

To begin with they briefly examined Charles Meik, the aptly named assistant to Sir Thomas Bouch, and there was some fine wrangling between him and counsel about whether he had or whether he had not all of Bouch's plans with him that afternoon. It was proved that he had not, not all of them, just 'some of them,' and he was smartly told to bring the lot by Monday.

The rest of the seven witnesses were the men who had opened the drama six days before.

James Watt and Signalman Thomas Barclay, trying to remember what each had seen and done in that wind-locked signal box on the Wormit bank. Signalman Somerville, explaining how he had stared out along the bridge, looking for the train that never came. Station-agent Morris, the ticket-collector Friend, the porter Ingles, recalling their last sight of the 5.20 from Burntisland as it left St Fort into the rain and the wind.

Then it was late in the afternoon and Mr Trayner, for the Board of Trade, with an air of asking the Court's pardon, said that he would be calling 'a better class of witness' on Monday when the Court reassembled.

The public left with a flat sense of anti-climax. as if it had believed that in one afternoon the whole story of the disaster would have been told, and that there would have been an explanation of why the bridge had fallen. There had been no reality in those dry questions and answers. There was a greater reality in the verses the ballad-sellers were calling through the lamplight.

> 'Slowly creeping, swiftly dashing,
> Now the train mid-stream is nearing ...'

The public read its evening newspapers, and was told that

Diver Watts had come to the surface that afternoon with a foot-warming pan. Another diver had found a piece of piping full of telegraph messages. Diver Simpson, groping in the darkness, had touched something soft that had turned out to be not a body but just another cushion.

The whalers were searching the mouth of the firth and the rim of the sea around the coasts of Fife and Forfar. The fishermen and the mussel-dredgers had taken the shores of the lower reaches. Captain Bremner, Chief Constable of Fife, had placed forty constables on duty to prevent demonstration, looting, and any other abominable excess should a body be found.

The refreshment-room at Tay Bridge Station was now equipped with tables on which the flotsam was laid.

A Balmoral bonnet, a gentleman's blue scarf, a cuff knitted in mauve and black wool – all found by Constable James Cooper at Stannergate, where a wash of the beach jutted out into the tide.

A silk umbrella, child's cotton sock, and a velvet shoe. A cloth cap with paint stains, a woman's chemise, and a felt hat, small enough to belong to a child.

At dusk on Saturday night the master of the *Armitus*, on passage from North Shields to Burntisland, saw the top of a railway carriage floating with the tide five miles north of Berwick. Not having heard of the disaster, he recorded the incident in his log and let the carriage-top float on.

Sunday was a great day in the pulpits.

A great day to explain that, whereas death was man's lot, just how it might come to him depended on the Lord's mercy.

In Edinburgh, a Free Church minister, Dr Begg, cried out 'If there is one voice louder than others in this terrible event it is that of God! Determined to guard his Sabbath with jealous care.'

'God,' said Dr Begg, 'does not afflict except with good cause. The Sabbath of God has been dreadfully profaned by our great public companies. These wicked people are actually going to have the audacity to rebuild this bridge.'

Nor did the minister believe that the seventy-four men, women and children still below the Tay waters were entirely guiltless. 'Is it not awful to think that they must have been carried away when many of them must have known that they were transgressing the Law of God?'

If they had been attending to the Word of the Lord they would have been at home, or in the kirk, and certainly not in a train on the Sabbath.

Throughout Scotland all Sabbatarian ministers preached on this theme.

'The fall of the Tay Bridge,' cried the Rev. George Macaulay at Roxburgh Free Church, 'can be classed with the wars in Afghanistan and Zululand as a token of God's displeasure. God has been speaking to us, and now he is speaking by the voice of events near to every one of us.'

The hand of God, said Mr Macaulay, had been seen in the destruction of the unfortunate passengers because of 'the systematic desecration of that day which God has set apart for Himself.'

Scottish newspapers reported such sermons, or did not report them, and left it at that. If anyone wished to disagree they might do so in the correspondence columns, but it was not profitable for editors to instruct their readers in theological common sense. But in England *The Times*, writing for Anglicans, could mock without offence. It quoted from the sermons and said:

It will be felt that they exhibit in a peculiar light at once the credulity and illogical ruthlessness of these persons, for they must need believe that if the railway company abolishes Sunday trains it will be needless to make the bridge stronger, and that the thousand who travel on week-days will be safer on it than the hundred who travel on the Sabbath. It is a curious comment.

It was a curious comment, but only in England. In Scotland people could believe that the fall of a bridge was God's judgement. How else was His anger to be made manifest? They could believe that Jessie Bain, with her sweetheart's letter in her muff, suffered death for the sin of using wheeled transport on the Lord's Day. The imaginatively religious mind accepted the awful hand of God more easily than it understood the bad workmanship of an iron founder, or the misjudgement of a civil engineer.

Even where some ministers realized that the bridge must have fallen from its own weakness their conclusions could have been of small comfort to Sir Thomas Bouch, sitting alone in his hotel room that Sunday.

The Reverend Mr Macrae of Dundee pointed out that if fever and pestilence were God's judgement on dirt and bad drainage, so might the Tay Bridge Disaster be a blessing in disguise, leading to the building of another bridge of greater security.

# VII

*'In the name of outraged feelings!'*

ON Monday, 5 January 1880, one week after the disaster, Dundee woke to life with the belch of smoke and steam from the jute factories, with great explosions of flame in the shipyards, with the gas lamps blinking out one by one on the rising streets behind the city, and with the bells of Old Steeple ringing. Snow lay on the top of the Sidlaws, a thin white line drawn uncertainly across the grey sky. Then the daylight was suddenly strong and harsh, and the divers came down the frosty cobbles to work on the river.

This was the eighth day, and, if the whalers were to be believed, the lost dead would now rise to the river's surface for Christian burial.

In the Sheriff's Court Mr Rothery, Mr Barlow, and the Colonel assembled again to hear evidence of the disaster. There was a smaller crowd in the Court this day, mostly idlers who would not work, and gentlemen who needed not. The air was cold, and for half an hour or more there was a strange rustling accompaniment to the sound of voices, as this man or that rubbed the palms of his hands together to warm his chilled blood.

Once more Charles Meik was called, and was asked by Mr Trayner if he had now brought *all* of Sir Thomas' plans. Mr Meik said 'I have brought all I can find' and he was allowed to withdraw, never, he hoped, to be called again.

The weather outside was favourable, and the *Fairweather* left the Tidal Basin early. Aboard her were the brother and brother-in-law of the dead guard David Johnston. There were many newspapermen too, most of them Englishmen, struggling to catch the words and meaning of the answers given them in hard Doric. A few felt the uneasy heave of the river, and they looked unhappily towards the clouds that were gathering above a spur of the Ochils like a waiting army.

The *Fairweather* was moored to the fourth of the fallen piers, and diving commenced.

Many little boats had been out on the river before dawn, fishing-boats and mussel-dredgers, with bearded men in Balmoral bonnets leaning over the stern with dragging lines. The sound of their lingering calls came lazily through the still air.

About the time that Mr James Lawson was telling the court that he had seen 'a mass of fire fall from the bridge,' a grappling line which had been thrown over the starboard side of one of the fishing-boats was held fast by something on the bottom.

There was a cry of '*A buidy!*', which was taken up from boat to boat. The other boatmen turned from their own dredging and rowed towards the spot. The cry reached the shore and passed through the city, and a crowd came clattering down the cobbles to the Tidal Basin. In Tay Bridge Station the waiting, still waiting relatives stood up quickly and hurried out.

Guard Johnston's brother Andrew asked if he could be put ashore, and Harbour-master Robertson had him rowed there, and the brother-in-law too. But now the grappling line had been hauled inboard the fishing-boat, and attached to the end of it was a baulk of timber only. The fishermen stood up in the boat and waved their arms and shook their heads, but nobody ashore believed them or understood them.

An hour later the same fishing-boat hauled in a body.

It was quickly wrapped in a blanket and taken to a ferry-steamer moored to the dock. The police fought to keep the crowd from the quayside. Black-clothed relatives were pushed this way and that and they were the only people there who were not crying out. At last the body was taken to the refreshment-room at Tay Bridge Station, and laid on a wagon-sheet with the face uncovered. It was a man. The relatives walked towards it slowly, looking down and hurrying on until Andrew Johnston came and looked down, and did not move on.

The body was his brother David. It was not disfigured, and the expression on the face was natural and placid, although there was a little blood on the right ear. David Johnston's fists were clenched, and this was the only sign of anguish or fear about him. There was £1 13s. 6d. in the pocket of his uniform, and his silver watch had stopped at 7.16.

Andrew Johnston wept, and still weeping went to find his brother's widow.

Six divers were down on the river bed that day, including a strangely selfless man called Henry Watt, and although they discovered much about rivets and iron, about the position of the train and the fall of the High Girders, they found no more bodies. The whalers hauled up a foot-rug, a cotton handkerchief, and a felt hat. When the sun went down, shortly after four o'clock, the crowd went home under the gas lamps. In the darkness of the refreshment-room David Johnston waited for the attention of Smith & Sons.

Ordinary people argued in their homes or in the taverns. But the proper mouthpiece for gentlemen was the correspondence column of the *Advertiser*. They dipped their nibs. Why, asked Mr Thomas Green, was there no telephonic communication between the divers and the boats? Surely a telephonic contrivance could be fixed inside the divers' helmets? Mr David Williamson said he had rowed up to the barge that afternoon and had been invited aboard by a gentleman of his acquaintance. He had been appalled to discover that the divers had to *feel* their way about the river bed in total darkness. Why could not they have lights down there?

As the Archdeacon of Glasgow sat down to dinner that night his servant brought in a letter. It was damp, and the stiff paper tore easily as the Archdeacon opened it. The servant said 'I'm sorry it's a' wet, sir, but it's been in the Tay.'

For all that the Archdeacon was still able to recognize the signature and read the handwriting of his dear friend Mr Gladstone.

In the witness box at the Court on Tuesday morning James Young, a carriage inspector in the employ of the North British Railway, was asked if he had examined the train at Burntisland on the afternooon of 28 December. He said that he had, having tapped the wheels and examined the axle-boxes and springs and couplings.

Mr Barlow: Have you ever known a carriage blown over by the wind?

Witness: No.

Nobody who was asked this question had ever seen a carriage blown over by the wind.

Morning and afternoon the Court heard evidence from the divers, who spoke of the things they had seen and done below the Tay water, and their simple answers, made without exaggeration, vividly painted the darkness below the river, the swirl of mud and sand, the heavy movement of arms and legs, and the cold, the terrible cold.

Thus Charles Tate, explaining that he had been a diver for eighteen years and had come to Dundee after Harbour-master Robertson had guaranteed his expenses, said

'I hove away down to the place where I thought would be the best, and still made circles round and tried in the circle. Then I would wait a little and made other circles, and I found some lamps. I found a cord hanging down, that came across my hand in making these circles. I went up it to the first-class carriage door. The window was open or had been broken, but in placing my hand over I found the roof was off, so in place of going in by the door I went in by the roof. I took the cord and what I understood to be a parasol or an umbrella, and tied them up and sent them up by my line.'

Henry Watt, who was this selfless diver from Sunderland, told the Court how he had found a third-class carriage in darkness, and on his hands and knees had crawled the whole length of it, and 'found nothing at all'. The flooring on which he crawled had been entire and upright, which meant that the carriage was not lying on its side but standing on its wheels in the mud and the gravel.

John Barclay explained how he had come from North Shields to get work when he heard there was a call for divers in Dundee. Dugald Drummond had taken him into the employ of the Railway Company, and he had gone down on the morning of Thursday. He described how he had found the couplings of a carriage underneath a girder (using his broad hands to show the Court how the girder had been lying at an angle of 45°). He had crawled underneath this with his cable and airline trailing after him, and the bubbles of his breathing going up to the surface.

On Sunday he had gone down farther north. 'I went down between the girders, and I thought I put my hand into the funnel of the engine, but the tide was too strong. I was in a confused mass trying to get out; and I could not give a proper statement whether it was a funnel or not.' Which was how he calmly described his fear.

All the divers were asked if they had found a girder broken, for this was a question of great importance, and most of them had not. But John Cox, who was the Harbour diver, said that on the previous Monday he had gone down about 20 feet and south of the fourth pier 'I found a girder broken there.'

Mr Trayner: It is broken right through and separated?

Witness: Right through, a clean break.

He said that the water had been thick and muddy and it had been difficult to see anything. He had felt with his hands, along fifty feet of the girder in muddy darkness.

Simpson, too, had found a broken girder, broken clean across he said, and he opened his hands to indicate a gap of about 18 inches. And he said that the engine and tender, and all the carriages he had discovered beneath the water, were still inside their cage of girders.

Four bodies were found that Tuesday, embedded in the sand close to the bridge, and were dragged free from it by grappling irons.

Between six and seven in the morning, before first light, a hundred men went out on to the river to continue the search. The water was unusually smooth, and close inshore it was possible at times to see the river-bed quite clearly. A new form of trawl was being used. It consisted of an iron bar, 3 feet long and acting as an anchor to a line on which were fastened stout hooks. It was lowered to the river from whale-boat No. 13, and dragged along the river bed. Shortly before noon the men using it hailed the shore. They had caught something.

This something was hauled reverently aboard. It was James Leslie, the young timber clerk of Dundee, and in his pocket was his prize copy of Longfellow's poems, and his pencil-case and his ruler. They took him to Tay Bridge Station.

A boatman found another body that afternoon, the body of William Jack, the young grocer who had been visiting his re-cently-widowed mother at Dairsie. And later still, just before sunset, the whaleboats found the bodies of the ploughman James Crichton, and the moulder Robert Watson.

Clouds were pulling up over the city from the west, and covering the city with a leaden darkness as these two bodies were taken ashore. All the boats came in, a funeral armada, and there was a great silence on the river, until a cry came from the Esplanade.

The crowd there had seen another body floating. It was a woman's body. A young man leaped from the wall and in his clothes swam out toward it. But the cold was too great for him and he turned back, while the body sank again.

Long after sunset a boy came running to his home in Stan-nergate, with a letter and a silk umbrella which he had found on the beach. The letter was still legible. It said *'My dear Father – I intend coming home on Sunday night with the 7.30 train. Hoping you are well and merry. Love to all.'*

It was the letter which Jessie Bain had forgotten to post.


The body of Robert Watson lay in a coffin at the far end of the refreshment-room. His four brothers came on Tuesday even-ing to identify him, and when the lid was lifted they saw 'The expression of great pain on his face.'

Three of the brothers stood and looked and did not move, but the fourth brother, who was blind, knelt by the coffin and gently passed his hands over the dead man's face. He said *'It's Rabbie!'* and wept.


Mr William Smith, of Smith & Sons, cabinet-makers and

undertakers, made himself personally responsible for the mortuary in the refreshment-room.

On Wednesday evening one gas-jet only burnt at the far end, its ruddy, uncertain light falling on seven black coffins that lay against the left side of the room. Their lids were on, but had not been screwed down. On each lid was a card, and on this card Mr Smith had written the occupant's name in a neat copper-plate.

Along the marble-topped counter, 'recently bright with sparkling crystal', railwaymen were quietly ticketing articles that had been found in the pockets of the dead, or had been washed-up ashore. These were then placed on shelves. Against the wall that faced the coffins was a line of caps and coats and umbrellas and handbags and elastic-sided boots. There were many elastic-sided boots.

Behind a folding-screen at the far end of the room two women were stripping the sanded clothes from the last body to be brought in that day. This was the stoker of No. 224, John Marshall. He had come to the surface of the Tay 400 yards from the southernmost of the broken piers. He had obviously died horribly, flung violently against the fire as the flames tongued out. His face was scorched black. There were two deep wounds on his head, his teeth were clenched and his lips were drawn back. There was no one to identify him, no kin that is, for his brothers had waited a week in Dundee and had then gone home, thinking that he would never return from the Tay. But Stationmaster Smith had recognized him, for all those terrible burns.

Wednesday had brought more bodies from the river. There was William Macdonald, the sawmiller of Blackness Road. His silver watch was still in his pocket, and so was his whistle and his watchkey. There was David Neish, the Lochee schoolmaster. There was the joiner John Sharp, the confectioner's apprentice William Threlfell (whose wet hymn-book lay on a shelf behind the counter), and there was Walter Ness, the saddler.

The Relief Fund had now reached £3,200, and Mrs Watson (who was the mother of the man David Watson and whose mind had become temporarily unhinged) was given immediate aid from it. In from the parish of Kettel came the Reverend Mr

Gordon who explained to Provost Brownlee that the ploughman Crichton had been the sole supporter of his mother and two sisters. Relief was granted them too.

In weak, uncertain handwriting, set down only at the cost of much physical pain, Andrew Spence, a weaver of Newburgh, wrote to say that he and his wife, both aged seventy, had come to Dundee for news of their daughter Annie, who had died on the train. They were without funds, and were given money.

Driver Mitchell's widow was also without money, but 'the poor widow was extremely grateful for the sum sent her by Lord Inveruir'.

The newspapermen were going home. There was nothing to hold them in Dundee now. The Board of Trade Inquiry had adjourned on Tuesday, 6 January, with the decision to assemble again in London at a later date.

It had been a triumph for the Press. Journalists from London, Liverpool, Manchester, Sheffield, Edinburgh and Glasgow, had arrived in Dundee early on Monday, 29 December. Many newspapers had sent as many as four special writers. Their competitive presence in Dundee, filling the rooms of the Royal Hotel, had driven the local press to unprecedented endeavours. A complete verbatim report of the first day's evidence at the Court of Inquiry (which closed at five p.m.) had been edited and printed by the *Dundee Advertiser* and sent on its way south to London and Manchester by six o'clock.

The staff of the General Post office, through which the visiting corps of newspapermen had filed their stories, had worked fifteen hours a day. The Postmaster slept in his office and called for extra help from the postmasters and mistresses of Broughty Ferry, Monifieth and Carnoustie.

Five fast Wheatstone instruments were kept in action at the rate of one hundred words a minute, being fed by ten 'punchers' for perforating the ribbon, after which the messages were transmitted automatically. In the first week enough copy to fill 250 columns of an ordinary newspaper was sent out of Dundee daily.

Since this was syndicated material the published figure was nearer 1,000 columns.

The heaviest day's work at the Post office was on Monday, 5 January, at the end of the second day of the Inquiry. One hundred thousand words were filed through the Telegraph Office.

The artists of the *Illustrated London News* and the *Graphic*, who had spent sickening days on the river-boats in order to make their drawings of the broken bridge and tossing boats, rode in fast carriages to Perth, exhausting drivers and winding horses, so that they might put their sketches on the London trains.

And then, when the story lost its major importance, as it slipped down the columns of the world's Press before more urgent news, the newspapermen went home, and left the rest of the coverage to the resident linage men.

On Thursday afternoon the crew of a whaler off Stannergate saw the body of a woman rising gently to the surface on their starboard side. They rowed to it and a seaman leant over and grasped the trailing hair. The body turned and sank, and left only a tortoise-shell comb in the seaman's hand. There were many such combs lying on the shelves in the refreshment-room.

Before the magistrates at Broughty Ferry came David Knight, a fisherman, accused of finding and keeping a hamper containing a turkey, a hare, a brace of partridges and other game and also of finding and keeping a cushion from a first-class carriage. He was invited to choose between a fine of ten shillings or seven days' imprisonment. He chose to pay, and made apologies.

The Dundee Police Commissioners met and discussed the bridge, and warmly greeted Baillie Macdonald's suggestion that the directors of the North British Railway should receive 'expressions of deepest sympathy in this terrible and unequalled calamity'. It was earnestly hoped that the Company would build another bridge as soon as possible. They did not add that they also hoped Sir Thomas Bouch would have nothing to do with its design, but, less publicly, everybody else was saying so.

He had been chosen as a scapegoat. Few people waited for the report of the Court of Inquiry to discover whether Bouch could be justly blamed or not. Someone must be responsible for the fall of the bridge, and for so many dead, and who else but the man who designed it? Now it was necessary for those who had once been fulsome in their praise of Bouch and his bridge to return rapidly to their earlier scepticism. It was a fortunate man who could produce some evidence of the fact that he had always been against the bridge. Mr James Littlejohn had frequently said, and could be proved by witnesses to have said, that he had 'an invincible belief that a structure at once so lean and so long and lofty, and founded among shifting sands, carried so high in the air without buttress or side-stays of any kind, must break down'.

He died before the bridge did break down, but his relatives claimed that 'he was haunted to the last with the misgiving that the structure would not sustain the full weight of a westerly gale'.

So the eight years' fight, the struggle against the 'nasty jabble' of jumping seas, the cylinders rolling and falling on their crews, the exploding air-bells, the men dead and drowned in the sand, the cement bursting the caissons, the cheerful lectures of Albert Groethe, the carillons and huzzas, the lunches and the banquets, all this had been for nothing, and in Dundee during that January of 1880 no one could be found who had ever had the slightest faith in the bridge.

On Thursday, 8 January, four more bodies were recovered. Archie Bain was brought ashore by a whale-boat under the command of James Cummings. Bain had risen to the surface three hundred yards east of the bridge. His ruddy face was further discoloured and, like so many of the dead, his fists were tightly clenched. Volunteer boats also brought in Thomas Davidson (a ploughman) and Alexander Robertson. They were carried to Mr Smith's mortuary where, on the shelves, lay a row of gold and silver watches, and all of them stopped at 7.13, or 7.16, or 7.27, or times like these.

The crew of the *Grace Darling*, a lifeboat that had been rowed all the way from Bamburgh in Northumberland to take part in the search, found the body of James Henderson, the sawyer's son, and in his pocket was the letter from his sister's sweetheart. The girl found it awaiting her when she came to identify her brother's body.

Boat-hooks and irons grappled with the bodies of three more women as they rose to the surface that day, but each of them refused to leave the river, and turned over and floated away and sank, leaving a handkerchief or a tortoiseshell comb adrift on the water.

A Mr Joshua wrote to all the newspapers to say that he was only waiting for the word to supply one hundred electric lamps to aid the search at night. But no one sent him the word.

On Friday morning, quite early, when there were strands of mist, like wind-blown wool, entangled in the standing girders of the bridge, a seaman in a whale-boat found the body of David Watson, aged nine, a quarter of a mile from the bridge. There was nothing at all in his pockets, and probably had never been, for he was wearing his best clothes and had been told not to spoil them. His mother prayed at the boy's side with her four brothers-in-law.

It was a bad day out on the river. Through the driving rain could be seen the twelve empty piles of the broken bridge, tufted with white spray. The volunteer boats did not go out, but the whalers did, and danced there, until the heaving water released the body of William Peebles, the land steward of Corrimony. It was brought to the refreshment-room and laid on a tarpaulin awaiting one of Mr Smith's black coffins. The steward's day-book and gun licence were placed on the shelves.

William Peebles left a widow and eight children, and his sister fainted when she saw his body.

The whalers also found the body of Davie Macdonald, aged eleven, and he was brought to the station at the same moment as his father (who had been recovered on Wednesday) was being buried. The boy was identified by an uncle, and Station-master Smith wrote in the mortuary inventory 'On the boy Macdonald – one penny pencil.'

George Johnston came to the water's surface too, the young

man who had fought the wind along the platform of St Fort as he looked for Eliza Smart. By the closest reckoning the lovers could not have spent more than eight minutes together in the train.

In Aberdeen, the Chamber of Commerce passed a motion of sympathy with the North British Railway Company, and speeded it along with the hope that the company would soon build a new bridge as it was of greatest importance that Aberdeen should be in direct communication with the south by an eastern route. Their impatience could be reasonably explained. The bridge had cut the journey from Aberdeen to London from 18 hours to 13, and having enjoyed this for so many months the thought of returning to older discomforts was distasteful.

This anxious sympathy for the North British Railway was not universal. A correspondent, signing himself 'One of the Mourners', wrote to the *Advertiser*:

Evidently the Directorate of the North British Railway Company is so engrossed with defending their money interests and planning the rebuilding of their fallen structure that they cannot give thought or time how best the dead may be restored to their sorrowing friends. In the name of outraged feelings I call upon the Company to appoint a well-skilled engineer to take charge and secure the service of steam trawlers.

However, after the Aberdeen Chamber of Commerce had passed its resolution of sympathy some members had suggested that it might be in good taste to express sympathy with the relatives too. This was duly recorded in the minutes before another member moved 'Next Business'.

Three hundred wagon loads of wreckage had now been collected from the river shore seven miles below Dundee, between Harecraig and Monifieth. It was estimated that there would be nearly 400 loads before all the flotsam was gathered.

All the carriage wood, the roofs, doors, window frames, seats, cushions, were sent to the Company's works at Glasgow.

# VIII

ALL through the month of January, 1880, there were vessels on the river, fishing-boats and mussel-dredgers from Broughty Ferry, yachts from Newport, dinghies with volunteer crews, and the sight of them was now common-place. Even the recovery of a body no longer disturbed Dundee. The funerals, moving black on the wet cobbles, had relatives only for mourners. There was a limit to the grief which the majority of the public could show, and much of this had been expended on the funeral journey of Ann Cruickshank.

By the middle of the second week 25 men, women and children had been placed on the tarpaulin cloths in the refreshment-room, identified by their relatives and removed as quickly as possible by Mr Smith and his assistants.

The North British Railway closed West Newport Station, the fall of the bridge having made it useless. Closed too were the signal cabins at both ends of the bridge, and thus Signalmen Thomas Barclay and Henry Somerville were robbed of employment. There was much unemployment in Dundee which was blamed, not always with justice, on the fall of the Tay Bridge.

Diver Henry Watts refused to accept payment for his services.

The dragging and the dredging went on. The bodies of David Cunningham and Robert Fowlis were recovered one bright sunlit morning. These two stonemasons, who had been friends in boyhood, who lodged together in manhood, who travelled the same train, died in it, and were buried together in Kilmany kirkyard.

The Dundee Artillery Volunteers escorted the funeral procession of their comrade Robert Syme. And in a waiting-room at

Tay Bridge Station a short memorial service was held one evening for 'the boy Macdonald', he of the penny pencil.

There were still many people who wished to help in the recovery of the bodies, if not by spending long hours on the water with grapnels at least by writing well-phrased letters of advice to the press.

'Whenever you are assured,' wrote one . . .

. . . that your grapnel is fixed to the object keep a steady strain on the rope. Never slacken it for an instant, pull slowly, no sudden jerking, and when you are certain that the object is, say, within two yards of the boat lean over as far as you can, and when the object is, say, within a foot of the surface have a man ready to grasp it. I do so write under the impression that it is everyone's duty to advise and help another on this sad occasion.

'I am sure,' wrote another . . .

. . . that it would pay one of the enterprising photographers of Dundee to photograph one or two of the principal objects as they appear under the waters of the Tay and publish the photographs. I am sure they would sell, not only as representing the unfortunate parts of the famous Tay Bridge, but be a novelty, viz. – photographs taken under water. Enclosing my card, I am, Sir, yours truly, Amateur optician.

Another correspondent asked why the naval gunboats that were at anchor off the estuary mouth should not move up stream and fire their cannon across the water (unshotted, of course). It was well-known by nautical men that such a practice served to bring sunken bodies to the surface.

Not everyone thought of writing letters of advice. Some were stealing pieces of the wreckage for souvenirs. Constables therefore stood on guard at night, or walked the shores of Tayside with bull's-eyes at their belts.

A Mr David Cunningham proposed a special trawl which, he said, had been used, and very successfully. It consisted of a frame, built like a farmer's harrow, with teeth 'for drawing up the bed of the river and disturbing any sunken body'. The North

British Railway Company preferred to use its own methods. It now equipped two steam vessels with grappling irons of such weight that they ploughed up the bed of the river to a depth of more than one foot.

Mr Tweeney stayed on in Dundee. He was still waiting to take charge of Mr Benyon's body, and to pay £20 to anyone who discovered it, though how anybody could know where to look for one particular body Mr Tweeney did not explain. Harley repeated his promise to keep his eyes open below water for a well-built, well-dressed gentleman with a diamond ring, a plain buckle ring, and a Masonic scarf-pin.

Harley was, in any case, losing much of the esteem in which he had been held at the beginning. It was argued that he was not paying sufficient attention to his duties, these being to establish the exact position of train and girders for the information of the North British. On 14 January he went down into the mud-stained water and came up claiming that he had found part of a third-class carriage on the west side of the bridge, which was absurd.

A shoemaker called John Barclay (who must have been one of those extraordinarily bizarre characters that appear sooner or later on the scene of all calamities) hired a small yacht on the afternoon of Thursday, 15 January, and was seen sailing out in the cold sunlight towards the bridge. Sitting in the bow of his tiny vessel was a Highland woman wrapped in a grey plaid. The people on shore watched as the yacht tacked to and fro in response, it seemed, to the instructions of her waving arms.

The yacht returned shortly after sunset, and Mr Barclay explained what he had been about.

The lady, he said, was 'a person who described herself as a clairvoyant and a mesmerist'. She had approached Mr Barclay some days earlier and said that if he were prepared to take her out on the river she could, by means of her unusual powers, tell him where the bodies lay on the river-bed. He had accordingly hired the yacht and crew and taken her out. It was necessary, she explained to him, for him to mesmerize her before her powers could work, and she instructed him in the manner of this. Mr Barclay reported that he had been successful in placing her in a trance.

'I took her out and mesmerized her on the water. After that I asked her to point out to me in what part of the water there were bodies lying.'

The woman had pointed to the water ahead of the yacht and said that there was a man lying there. It was by the big sand hummock called Middle Bank, and she said that he was wearing a dark topcoat and dark trousers.

'Is there a watch on the body?' said Barclay.

'There is a watch on the body,' said the Highland woman.

'Look in the pockets, madam, and tell us what you see.'

She said 'There is silver in one pocket, and copper in the left-hand pocket.'

'Put the trawl out,' ordered Mr Barclay.

The trawl was put out, and it would not touch bottom. The yacht moved across the spot the Highland woman had indicated, but still the trawl could not touch the bottom. Mr Barclay looked at her, and she said: 'The water is too deep for the trawl to touch bottom.'

Mr Barclay put back to Dundee, while the Highland woman sat silently in the bow, except once when she looked back to the bridge and said: 'There are twenty bodies still in the High Girders.' An observation which Mr Barclay felt too disgusted to acknowledge.

Once ashore he said: 'Myself and my crew are dispirited at this want of success. I mean because we did not bring any bodies to the surface.'

The Town Council held another meeting, expressed more sympathy with the North British Railway, voted another £100 to the Relief Fund, and hoped that someone could think of a more speedy way of recovering the lost bodies.

At which Councillor Henderson stood up and expressed his concern at the way the Board of Trade Inquiry had been held. Certain witnesses residing in Dundee, he said, had not been called, and now he understood that the next meeting of the Inquiry would be held in London at some unspecified date. There were many gentlemen in Dundee who were prepared to affirm that trains had passed over the bridge at the extraordinary speed of 40 miles an hour.

He had also been informed that the vibration of trains travelling at such a rate had resulted in a number of the bolts on the bridge being shaken away. Why, he asked, were not the painters, who knew every inch of the bridge from north to south, called to give evidence?

The Provost agreed to call the attention of the Inquiry to these matters.

And out on the Tay the boats were still trawling in the strong wind and the rain. A young woman called at the mortuary and, through her tears, identified a felt hat as one belonging to her sweetheart, Robert Culross. Detective Henry Martin, of the Dundee Police, who was in charge of the mortuary, restored her from her swoon with strong spirits of ammonia.

Diver Harry Watts now gave two guineas to the Relief Fund.

The body of 'the boy David Watson' was buried one bleak afternoon beside his father. The rain ran in creamy rivulets from the banked soil into the tiny grave. And on the same afternoon Thomas Bouch made a rare appearance in the open. He went out on the river to watch the dynamiting of one of the sunken girders.

Ann Cruickshank had a last, post-mortal moment of notoriety. A rumour, which began in Dundee but which was never traced to its source, claimed that she had never been aboard the train at all. She had been murdered in Edinburgh and her body had been taken to the Tay and thrown there to make it seem as if she were a victim.

There were, of course, people who believed the rumour. Had her body not been found six days before the others?

The police made their investigations, and from what they were told by Lady Baxter's coachman (he who had arrived too late for Ann and Eliza to catch an earlier train), and from what they were told by Station-agent Morris of St Fort, they decided that Ann Cruickshank had not, after all, been the victim of foul play, unless it was considered that what the bridge and the storm did to her had been foul enough.

Mrs Robert Watson came away from the funeral of her boy David and gave £1 of the money granted her by the Relief Fund to each member of the boat's crew that had recovered her son.

On the following morning the body of her other son, the boy Rabbie, was washed up on the beach.

The Town Council, pricked on by Press and public, went aboard one of the steamers to satisfy itself and the city that the work of recovery was being carried out efficiently. It believed that this was the case, but it suggested to the North British Railway that since most of the bodies had been recovered by small boats the Company should employ some of their own, and pay the crews 2s. 6d. a day, plus £1 to be divided among them for every body found. It also asked the Broughty Ferry fishermen to come up river and drag their lines near the bridge.

The fishermen came, and they found the body of Robert Culross.

Early in the morning of 19 January there were two explosions along the southern end of the girders, explosions that raised a slow-falling column of spray above the Fifeshire horizon and brought the people of Dundee from their doors, fearing that more of the bridge had fallen. But the Company was merely using dynamite again to loosen the girders below water.

Mr Rothery, far off in London, heard of the dynamiting and sent an irritable telegram demanding that it cease forthwith. The Court of Inquiry wished Mr Valentine to take some underwater photographs of the girders for use as evidence. If the North British continued to displace these girders such photographs would be useless. Mr Valentine was taken out to the bridge with his equipment. He had powerful electrical lamps to illuminate the river-bed, but he discovered that their light was diffused by the water – and that visibility below was three hundred times weaker than on a dull winter's day above. He abandoned the experiment, the Court of Inquiry was informed, and the dynamiting began again.

For the first time the mortuary was empty, the tarpaulin cloths vacant, and no coffins were lying along the left wall. Thirty bodies had been recovered from the water and buried in hillside kirkyards along Tayside, and the date of their death and the manner of their dying was being chipped into head-stones.

But the search went on. The crews of 36 mussel-dredgers were being paid 3s. 6d. a day by the North British Railway (which evidently thought the Town Council's suggestion of 2s. 6d. too niggardly) and it offered £2 for every body recovered (having further thought that its original offer of £5 was too extravagant).

The Perth Council, hearing that the Company was proceeding with plans for a new bridge, sent a sharp note of reminder and protest. It had been told, it said, that these plans were for a bridge just above the level of the water. Against such a fantastic proposal it could not object enough. If it were built no ship would ever be able to sail up to the ancient capital of Scotland.

Diver Harley, already in partial disgrace because of his claim that part of the train lay on the west side, went down again late in January and came up claiming that he had seen bodies lying in the mud. He was asked to dive again the next day, and he did so, and came up saying that he could see nothing. There appears to be no explanation for his extraordinary behaviour, for he was a fine diver, and much respected before the fall of the bridge.

By the end of January 33 bodies had been recovered, and one of the last of these was pretty little Bella Neish, the schoolmaster's daughter. She was found one frosty morning, lying on the beach below Dundee, and it is a strange thing that of the four female bodies that were recovered from the Tay only one was an adult.

From then on only occasionally was a body found, with many days' interval between them, until the fishermen and mussel-dredgers went back to their work, and what bodies were found came to the surface of their own volition.

One hundred and sixteen days after the disaster a body washed up on the Caithness shore was identified as a passenger of the train. It had travelled a long way. Four days later another body, barely distinguishable as that of a man, was found a short distance east of the *Mars*. It was the last to be found.

Twenty-nine were never recovered, and lie somewhere still in the mud and the sand of the Firth of Tay.

In Spring, in April when the river was serene and sunlit, divers Cunningham and Tait went down to engine No. 224 and made chains fast about her.

A steam-winch on the lighter *Henry* was set in motion, dragging her free from the grip of the gravel, so that the water boiled up above her. But before she was halfway to the surface the river stirred itself resentfully. The tide caught at the lighter and dragged it downstream with the engine swinging below water. A little to the west of Tayport lights the cables snapped, and 224 sank to the river-bed again.

A week later she was dragged ashore and beached, and lay there until the sea-air turned her green to red and her brass to green, and children played over her broken body.

# IX

## *'Beaumont Egg'*

LATE in February the Board of Trade Inquiry returned to Dundee for the examination of further witnesses, and this it had intended to do without the prompting of Councillor Henderson.

On the first day of the hearing, which was Thursday, 26 February, Mr Rothery patiently explained why he and his colleagues had been so long in coming. They had wished to wait for the spring tides so that they might examine the fallen bridge more satisfactorily. After testily pointing out to some objectors that he could not possibly 'lock up' witnesses until they gave evidence, Mr Rothery declared the opening of the 'Court of Inquiry upon the Circumstances attending the Fall of a Portion of the Tay Bridge'.

The principal witnesses who had clamoured to give evidence were, of course, those gentlemen who, busy with watch and pencil and paper, had timed the speed of trains across the High Girders and found it grossly in excess of 25 miles an hour.

There was William Robertson, the ex-provost of Dundee, and John Leng the publisher-editor. There was George Hume the ship's chandler, and Alexander Hutchinson the architect. All men highly respected in the city of Dundee. Mr Robertson described how he had once estimated the speed to be 42.4 miles an hour, and he explained that it was after this alarming experience that he abandoned his railway season ticket and returned to the ferry-boats. Mr Hutchinson, too, spoke of his 'mental discomfort', and of his belief that the movements of the bridge in high winds loosened the girders.

Whereupon the North British Railway Company offered the evidence of Mr Herman Quosbarth. Mr Quosbarth was Consul of the German Empire in Dundee, and he said that he had travelled on the bridge from its opening to its fall, and never once had he felt the slightest discomfort or apprehension. He had never travelled at 40 miles an hour through the High Girders, he had never experienced the slightest movement in the bridge. Mr Quosbarth was very happy in his memories of the bridge.

Station-master Smith, when recalled, said that he well remembered the protests that had been made to him by Mr Robertson, Mr Leng and others. A conscientious man, he had gone out to the bridge to test this claim of movement in the girders, and it was true that he had noticed 'a vertical motion', but nothing to alarm him. He had not reported any of the complaints to his superior officers because he had been unable to substantiate, from his own experience, these speeds of 40 and 42 miles an hour. When Mr Robertson made a second complaint Station-master Smith crossed and recrossed the bridge a dozen times, and he watched trains crossing and recrossing, and at the end of it all he had discovered nothing to confirm Mr Robertson's charges. So he did nothing, beyond passing on the complaint to the locomotive foreman.

'I was always watching the trains,' said Station-master Smith.

John Black, a clerk in the parcels office of the Caledonian Railway, had frequently crossed the Tay Bridge, and he had done so on the last train across before the Fall. He remembered, with some feeling, how the sparks had sprayed from the wheels of the brake van in which he was riding with Robert Shand. He had looked at them from the window and grown afraid. When the train went round the bend to the High Girders he had felt 'a sudden shock driving the carriage over, and then it gained its perpendicular'.

Most of the witnesses examined at Dundee between 26 February and 3 March were what Mr Trayner, Counsel for the Board of Trade, would have described as 'the lesser classes'. They were railway workers and painters and riveters, workmen from the Wormit Foundry, men and boys from the girder gangs. From them it was hoped to obtain answers to two fundamental questions. Did the trains travel beyond the regulation speed? Was there shoddy workmanship at the Wormit Foundry?

The first question was answered with a bland, almost patronizing denial by the seven engine-drivers who were called. They were a reserved, intransigent body of men, suspicious of the Court and resentful of what they felt to be an attempt to blame the fall of the bridge on them. When they failed to understand a question, or were reluctant to answer it, they put their heads to one side and said '*Eh?*' Mr Rothery was patient with them, as were all counsel, but it was evident that these men sorely rasped the nerves of the Court.

They said:

'I found nothing unusual in the steadiness of the trains.'

'I am certain that I never went more than 25 miles an hour.'

'I never travelled at speeds exceeding 25 miles because I saw notices stuck up for-bye that.'

'Such a speed [40 *miles an hour*] could not be got out of a tank engine.' And this with a tight, condescending smile.

'The bridge was the smoothest bit of the road.'

'I do not know that I ever did the crossing below 5½ minutes or 6 minutes. I have seen it take 7 on a coarse morning.'

And John Anderson, for 16 years a driver of railway engines, told how he had heard of ex-Provost Robertson's complaints.

'Mr Smith said to me, "John, Mr Robertson is complaining to me just now about some trains he came across with some days past that their speed is about 40 miles an hour." I said nothing to Mr Smith, but smiled to myself, I considered it perfect nonsense.'

Locomotive Foreman James Roberts, he who had crawled on hands and knees to the gap on the night of the disaster, was loyal to his drivers. He agreed that it was possible to get up to a speed of 40 miles an hour on the bridge, but *not*, he said, if it had to slow down to two miles an hour at each end to collect or deliver the baton. And without this ritual of the baton no train had been able to cross the bridge.

The united front of engine-drivers and foreman was impressive, but from gentle cross-examination emerged one disturbing fact that mocked all others.

The early morning trains from Newport to Dundee had been in the habit of racing the ferry-boats across the river.

None of the drivers who were examined would admit that he had ever driven his engine in such a race, but it seemed that all knew what happened. If morning train and morning ferry left Newport for Dundee at the same time ('Chock and block, every morning full') then the train would arrive before the boat, that is in ten minutes. If the train were late, however, it had to put on greater speed to match or beat the ferry. Passengers by boat and train (who did not share the alarm of Mr Robertson or Mr Leng) appear to have enjoyed this boyish contest.

The workmen from the Wormit Foundry appeared before the Court on Saturday, 28 February. Here were ill-educated, disinterested men without the skill to sustain a lie under cross-examination, and indeed without the wish to. They came into the Court in thick, coarse clothes, the skin of their hands and faces ingrained with iron-dust. They stared with a bewildered gravity at the Court and the counsels and the reporters. And they talked about Beaumont's Egg.

Indeed they talked so much about it that often it seemed that all that had held the bridge together had been this magic, malleable substance. It had been used to plug the blown-holes, the faults in the iron castings, melted in and left there to harden. When rubbed smooth by a stone and painted over it was indistinguishable from the iron about it.

Beaumont's Egg was much used at the Wormit Foundry, and the man who issued it to the workmen was Fergus Ferguson the foreman moulder, or, as he described himself, 'the foreman of every person under the roof except the turners'. He had been a moulder for 22 years, that is from his fourteenth year, and he was still young and very proud. He had an authority beyond that of an ordinary foreman, because Henry Noble and Gerrit Camphuis, who should have exercised control of the foundry, knew little or nothing about iron-moulding. Against their ignorance Ferguson's knowledge seemed great, and they left the

works in his hands. As worker after worker stepped before
the Court to give evidence this 'foreman of every person under
the roof' was seen to have very weak hands.

Alexander Milne, a dresser at the foundry, said that he had
seen holes in the castings which were only half an inch across
on the outside, but which spread inside to two inches or more.
These had been filled with Beaumont Egg. He had seen iron
columns go on to the lathe 'quite whole apparently and honeycombed after they were taken out'. They were not discarded
because of the faults but 'the honeycombed holes were generally filled up with the same combustible, Beaumont Egg, and
the columns laid down with others to go to the bridge'.

And he was asked what was this Beaumont Egg made of?

'It is composed of beeswax, fiddler's rosin, and the finest iron
borings melted up, and a little lamp black.'

'Is it when used a kind of paste, or is it fluid?'

'It is quite hard, and it will break like metal.'

'How do you put it in?'

'You take a red hot bar and melt it in.'

'And then it hardens like metal?'

And so he was asked where he got this Beaumont Egg.

'In a little office Ferguson had, the foreman's office.'

'Did he give you the stuff?'

'Yes, when I asked for it.'

He said that the Beaumont Egg would not melt in the sun, but
a man might pick it out of the hole with the point of a knife if
he cared. And not all the faulty castings were thus botched with
this 'combustible'. Milne remembered that he had once seen
more than 40 columns so full of faults that Ferguson had
ordered them broken up.

But after the iron columns were painted, or covered with
white lead and grease to prevent rusting, could these disguised
holes be seen?

'If the column got a sudden shake it would fall out. Without
that it could not be seen, or not very easily be seen by anyone
that looked over it.'

Peter Tuite had been a foundry-worker for 26 years. He

worked on the bridge as a dresser, or at the casting furnaces. Oh yes, he had used Beaumont Egg, he had filled 'a good many holes'. It was always on hand, if not in Ferguson's office there was always some 'in a wee box that lay between the turning-shop and moulding-shop on a brick wall'.

Sometimes the holes were there after casting, sometimes there was a scab of burning iron which, when chipped off, left a hole, and Beaumont Egg was used on that.

But someone must have bought the Egg and brought it to the shop.

'I think it was a man called Tasker,' said Peter Tuite.

'Out of his own money?'

'I do not know.'

'Is it likely that he spent his own money?'

'No, I don't say that, I don't think he did.'

'Then he must have got the money from the foreman, or from somebody else.'

'Or from the firm,' said Peter Tuite.

So John Tasker was called, and came, and said that he had been employed at the foundry dressing the columns after they came out of the mould.

'What was the biggest hole you filled with Beaumont Egg?'

'I cannot say.'

'What was the diameter – an inch?'

'I cannot say that.'

'Give me your idea – tell me.'

'We filled up many a hole with Beaumont Egg.'

'Where did you get it?'

'I made it.'

'Of rosin, beeswax, lamp black, and iron borings? Where did you get the money to buy these things?'

'Mr Ferguson gave me the money to buy those things.'

He had seen hundreds of holes in the iron that was cast, and had seen them filled by Egg, painted and sent on to the bridge. He had seen a great many more iron columns too faulty to be used, and these he had seen broken up. How many? He could not say. A hundred, perhaps, two hundred?

'A great many I have seen broken up that were not fit to put out to the Bridge.'

Then came Mr Balfour, counsel for the North British Railway Company, and he said to John Tasker. 'Were you dismissed by Mr Ferguson?'

'Yes,' said John Tasker.

'Why?'

'He said I stopped too long off.'

'What were you doing off your work, were you drinking?'

'Yes.'

'Have you been drinking today?'

'Yes, somewhat,' said John Tasker, the maker of Beaumont Egg.

If this admission discredited him it could not destroy the picture of honeycombed iron being filled with beeswax and iron-dust, and being sent out to make a bridge. Too many other witnesses had corroborated Tasker's evidence.

When John Gibb, another dresser, was called he spoke of blown holes and Beaumont Egg also, and he remembered an occasion when he and other workmen had been told (by Ferguson) to throw tarpaulin pokes over some iron columns which had been so filled, and which were waiting to go out to the bridge.

'Why?'

'To hide them from the contractors or their engineers.'

From whom, for example?

'From Mr Groethe, or Mr Gilkes.'

Did any of these workmen think that what they were doing was wrong? Tasker had answered for all of them, perhaps, when the question was put to him. He replied 'I did not care. I did what I was bidden.'

And after all this what had Fergus Ferguson to say? Nothing. Nothing, because he had given his evidence *before* his workers said that he had authorized this or ordered that. So he spoke with a fine arrogance and a ready eagerness, and was very sure of himself.

How many columns had he broken up at Wormit because of defects? 'Say from 30 to 40 at a rough estimate.'

Had he sent out any defective castings to be built into the bridge? He had sent none.

Perhaps he would tell the Court the kind of defects that existed in the castings sometimes when they came out of the mould.

'I have seen a good many things,' said Fergus Ferguson and looked at the gentlemen who had never touched a hammer or worked in a foundry. 'In fact if I tried to explain it to you without your being a practical man you never could understand it.'

'We will try,' said Mr Rothery gently, 'for instance . . .?'

'For instance, the top part would give way, and I have seen them come out. The casting was defective and it was broken up. I have seen the snugs or lugs of them defective, and they were broken up many a time; in fact I have seen where they were scabbed, and I have seen it broken up. I have seen it, in fact, upon many mornings two broken up in one morning, and often four broken up in one morning.'

Thus he gave a picture of a good and conscientious foreman refusing to allow bad castings to be sent to the bridge. And perhaps he did not realize that he was also revealing the terrible wastage in the foundry. When Mr Trayner questioned him he admitted that his figure of '30 to 40 at a rough estimate' for the number of columns he had seen broken up was in fact nearer 60 or 70, and even this figure may have been an under-estimate.

It was an under-estimate, this was made plain as Mr Trayner pressed on with the question.

'Have we got, do you think, the whole of them if we say you broke up about a hundred columns?'

Fergus Ferguson did not think so.

'How many then?'

'I have broken up over a hundred columns.'

'How many more?' insisted Mr Trayner.

'I have broken up, I suppose, for one defect or another about two hundred.'

Had he ever seen holes filled with Beaumont Egg? He had. 'I do not mind how often, but several times.'

'But I suppose you would not have authorized them to use it for a hole that was in your opinion dangerous?'

'Certainly not!' said Fergus Ferguson.

'Where was the Beaumont Egg kept?'

'I have seen the dressers keeping it.'

'I mean they had not to come to you for it every time they wanted it?'

Fergus Ferguson shook his head. 'No,' he said.

He was asked what he thought of the iron that was used for the columns of the bridge, and he said 'Well, I wouldn't like to say that it was the best, but as a general rule for ironbuilding work it was not what you'd call terribly bad iron.'

'Is that all you say for it?'

'The iron manufacturer must speak for himself.'

'But is that all you will say for it, that it is *not terribly bad iron*?'

'Eh?' said Fergus Ferguson, and Mr Trayner left the question at that.


When the Court sat again, in Westminster Hall on Monday, 19 April, it had a scale model of the bridge before it, and it heard the evidence of Henry Abel Noble, one-time assistant to Sir Thomas Bouch and latterly Inspector of the Tay Bridge.

He was perhaps the saddest figure in the whole Inquiry, a man not large enough to fit a tragic mould, nor small enough to escape pathos. A man without experience and with too much authority. A man whose greatest resolve seems to have been to save his employers money, so great, in fact, that he once undertook some river-diving himself rather than ask his company to find £3 a week for a professional diver.

No one but he was responsible for the bridge during the eighteen months it was in use. He started his duties with a crew of seven men and the use of the steamer *Tay Bridge*. A few months later he still had the steamer, but his men had been reduced to three. He worked diligently and unsparingly.

But against his giant responsibility his qualifications cut down his size to that of a mannikin.

'What were you bred to?'

'I was apprenticed to a bricklayer, and I worked myself out, and was taken by the Board of Works for nine years. The Metropolitan Board made me an inspector, and I am now an inspector of brickwork.'

'But you have no engineering skill?'

'I have no engineering skill.'

It must be repeated to be believed – a bricklayer who was the inspector of the longest, greatest railway bridge in the world, a bridge not of bricks but of latticed iron.

He had no orders from the company to inspect the iron columns, but being a conscientious man he took this duty upon himself, and perhaps it was as well that he did, for he found faults which even a bricklayer could not overlook. He found alarming slits in the iron of the columns on four piers, narrow slits it is true, wide enough to take the edge of a sheet of paper and nothing more. But they were slits five, six and even seven feet in length, and Henry Noble told Sir Thomas Bouch about them. The columns were strapped with bands of iron, and Sir Thomas seems to have regarded this as surgery enough, and who was Henry Noble to disagree?

He found, too, some cracks in the masonry of twelve of the piers, and these he reported to Bouch. They also were strapped. He found that the tidal pull had scoured the river-bed at the base of some of the piers and he had the scouring filled with rubble.

He found many gibs and cotters loose, but he told no one about these, but bought seven shillingsworth of iron with money from his own pocket and had the gibs and cotters packed. What iron was left over he gave to his workmen to make fire-pokers.

The more he told the Court of his eighteen months of supreme responsibility the more pitiable it became. After May, 1878 no one, no engineer, no contractor, no railwayman had come to inspect the bridge. He had no instructions to report any defects he found. He had no instructions to repair any defects he found. There was no one who had the responsibility of inspecting the ironwork from the platform to the masonry.

'No one was there to look after the ironwork of the bridge so far as it stood between the top of the pier and the bottom of the platform?'

'Except myself.'

'You had no instructions?'

'I had no instructions.'

He had the use of the *Tay Bridge* but no instruction with regard to finding stores for it.

'You did what you liked, if you thought it necessary for the purpose of the company.'

'Just so.'

'Did no one,' and this question was asked again and again, 'did no one inspect the bridge from the time you went there, which was in May 1878, till its fall in December 1879?'

'No one but me.'


Albert Groethe was called on 22 April, summoned from Spain where he was currently manager for the Tharsis Mines and Works. As he stood to give evidence his broad face was respectful and self-confident, his burly shoulders held back. His manner was as courteously deferential as if he were lecturing on the bridge to the members of the Glasgow Athenaeum.

It was his opinion, calmly given, that the bridge had been blown over by the force of the wind. He could think of no other explanation. Since he had been largely responsible for its erection this was an honest admission.

He was a civil engineer? Then what was the usual allowance for wind pressure?

'Upon this point,' he said, 'I think my notions have been very erroneous up to this time. They have been considerably modified by what I have heard since the Tay Bridge fell . . .'

At that moment he must have had a sobering recollection of past boasts, of confident assertions before clubmen and councillors.

He said 'I see, in my lecture, that I stated that the greatest wind that could ever be expected in this country was such a one as that in which the *Royal Charter* went down, when the pressure was 21 lb. to the square foot, and upon that calculation I pointed out that the stability of the bridge was undoubted.'

He was honest in all his admissions, even to the possibility of botching and poor workmanship. But he said: 'In a large work like this, where there were 600 or 700 men employed, and with all materials floating in barges, it was impossible to keep so strict an eye on everything personally as it would be in the same sort of work on the shore.'

And he said: 'I have never seen Beaumont Egg, as far as I know.' As for the quality of the iron used 'I am not a practical iron man.'

He was asked whether or not it had been true that no casting went out to the bridge that was not perfect, so far as he could tell from external survey. He said that this was so, and that he had given positive instructions to Gerrit Camphuis.

Not to the foreman?

'I recollect on one occasion particularly, having found a column in which a small hole had been filled with some foreign substance, being in company with Mr Gilkes, and the foreman was called and got a severe scolding for not having prevented this.'

But he was not a man of much experience in foundrywork? No he was not. Nor was Mr Camphuis? No he was not. Yet Mr Camphuis had been in sole charge of the foundry at one time? He had, but it had been administrative rather than technical charge.

Then who *did* have technical charge of the foundry?

Groethe spoke that name again, Fergus Ferguson, five syllables from a border ballad, and in speaking them he seemed to feel a resentment against the man that sharpened and shortened his answers.

'You told us that you once found a quantity of foreign matter in a defect and were extremely angry with the person that did it. Was that Fergus Ferguson?'

'Yes. He was responsible for it but he disclaimed all knowledge of it.'

'Then it is quite clear that all the columns did not pass even under his supervision?'

'*They must have done so!*'

Albert Groethe had once sincerely believed that there had never been a greater wind pressure in Britain than that which sank the *Royal Charter*. But this pressure of 21 lb. to the square foot was a feather blow compared with the figures mentioned by the meteorological experts called to Westminster Hall.

Sir George Airy, Astronomer Royal, admitted that he had given Thomas Bouch advice on wind pressure in 1873, when the engineer was making preliminary plans for a bridge across the Forth. He was careful to point out that he had never given advice about the weather in the Firth of Tay. What he did not know, and what it would seem Bouch did not tell him, was that Bouch considered this advice in relation to the Tay Bridge, then in its third year of construction.

Airy was a brisk and confident old man of seventy-nine, much given to exclaiming 'Oh, dear no!' in a high voice when replying to questions that struck him as particularly naive, and capable of the most adroit equivocation when faced by those that seemed too subtle to be innocent.

His advice to Bouch had been contained in a letter of 9 April 1873, and dated from Greenwich Observatory. It was produced and read to the Court. In it the Astronomer Royal said 'We know that upon very limited surfaces, and for very limited times, the pressure of the wind does amount to sometimes 40 lb. per square foot, or in Scotland to probably more.' He added, however, 'I think we may say that the greatest wind pressure to which a plane surface like that of a bridge will be subjected on its whole extent, is 10 lb. per square foot.'

He did not think that a pressure of 40 lb. or 50 lb. on a limited portion of a bridge span would be injurious. Such pressures, he thought, could be due to 'irregular swirlings of the air.'

When questioned he thought that the greatest known pressures in Britain in recent years had been 50 lb. or nearly so. He

thought that a heavy gale of December 1872 would have proved
this by his instruments, but 'unfortunately our recording pencil
broke at a particular point'. He had no way of telling what the
wind pressure might have been along the Tay on the night of
the Great Storm, because there were no instruments in Dundee.
It had, at its peak, been 10 lb. only at his 'constant residence in
Greenwich'.

Some of his confidence in wind pressures, and resistance to
them, appears to have weakened after the Tay Bridge fell, for he
wrote and published a paper on winds and bridges, and winds
that appeared to have blown bridges down. He wrote 'all calculations for the strength of a proposed structure should be
based on the assumption of a pressure of 120 lb. to the square
foot'. He called this 'establishing a modulus of safety'.

Counsel recalled this paper and asked the Astronomer Royal
if it were not true that 'until within a recent time, within the
last year or two, the knowledge and experience of engineers,
and of scientific men, did not suggest any such provision for
wind pressure?'

'I cannot say how it is,' said Sir George, 'but ideas do not
always come into one's mind.'

Thus his approach to bridge-building appears to have been
empirical. The maximum wind pressure that could be expected
was 50 lb. to the square foot, but since a bridge, built to withstand 10 lb., fell down it would be advisable in future to build it
in terms of 120 lb. to the square foot.

The gentlemen who followed the Astronomer Royal gave evidence in a manner that suggested that while the old man was no
doubt a great authority on astronomy, in meteorology he was a
child. Professor George Stokes, a professor of mathematics from
Cambridge, spoke of winds moving at 90 miles an hour, of pressures greater than 50 lb. to the square foot bearing down on
wide fronts.

Whereupon Mr Bidder, counsel for Sir Thomas Bouch, asked
the professor to agree that any engineer could be pardoned for
regarding the opinion of the Astronomer Royal as being of great
weight. He was promptly asked to withdraw the question.

The professor said that one should not think of gusts of great pressure being momentary whims of the wind. 'Sometimes they will go on for two or three minutes, blowing very heavily indeed.'

He was followed by Mr Henry Scott, Secretary to the Meteorological Council, who said that there most certainly could be heavy wind pressure down the Tay, along a front of perhaps 250 feet. This pressure could be more than 50 lb. to the square foot, and the velocity of the wind could be more than 90 miles an hour.

And when all this talk of winds and pressure was over it was announced that Sir Thomas Bouch would be called at half-past ten on the morrow.

At eleven o'clock in the morning of Friday, 30 April, the nineteenth and nearly the last day of the Inquiry, Sir Thomas Bouch began his evidence.

He was tired. He did not look well. Within his physical frailty, however, an obstinate if bewildered spirit was still in control. He gave most of his evidence without moving, looking at no one but his questioner. He had read none of the evidence so far given. He had read neither the newspaper reports nor the correspondence they had provoked. Consequently he must have been unaware of the growing feeling in the country that something had been terribly and criminally wrong with the bridge, with its design and with its materials. People were shocked by the thought that a foreman workman had been solely responsible for the foundry-work, that for the 18 months it was in use the bridge had been in the charge of a bricklayer. All the previous admiration for Bouch's achievements (which had reflected credit on the nation) had changed to a bitter sense of betrayal. There were even darker stories which the Court preferred to ignore until they forced themselves upon it.

Bouch's voice was low but firm as he answered the first conventional question put by his counsel, Mr Bidder.

'You are a civil engineer?'

'I am.'

And then, in his reply to the next question about the number of bridges he had built, there was a flare of defensive pride.

'I do not suppose anybody had built more . . .'

He gave evidence throughout the whole of Friday, and for most of Monday morning, and he was asked eight hundred and twenty questions by his counsel, by Mr Trayner, and by the three members of the Court. Most of his answers were prompt and calm. Only when he sensed the direction of a question, to determine the full extent of his responsibility, would his voice falter and did he cry out '*I do not know what more I could do!*'

But it soon became embarrassingly obvious that he had known little of what went on at the Wormit foundry, that he had not considered it his business to be there, or to ask questions there. This was not due to indifference or to laziness, but to the child-like faith he placed in others. He was a Cumberland man, and the contractors came from the north-west too, and he had faith in them with a parochial loyalty. So he left too much to men with too little experience. With scrupulous fairness, however, he refused to shelter behind them.

'Mr Noble,' he said, 'is one of the best examiners of concrete and Portland cement I have come across in my experience, and most careful.'

In the same manner he defended his assistant Allan Stewart, whose mathematical skill had translated Bouch's dreaming into practical realities.

'Mr Stewart had higher mathematical attainments than I had, and I was glad to get his assistance. Of course he went into them (*calculations of girder strains*) according to my directions and orders.'

Nor would he allow counsel to shake his faith in the type of bridge which he had chosen to build across the Firth of Tay. It was a design 'which I had found from 20 years' experience to be the best'.

It had been his bridge. There had been nothing wrong with it, in its design or its construction. It fell, but not because of its own faults. In those January days he had spent at Dundee he had formed his own opinion as to the cause of the disaster, and to his opinion he clung tenaciously.

'Well, I have thought about it very anxiously, and my opinion is fixed now; that it was caused by the capsizing of one of the last or the two last carriages – that is to say the second-class carriage and the van; that they canted over against the girder.'

Did he think that sufficient to destroy the bridge?

'I have no doubt of it. Practically the first blow would be the momentum of the whole train until the couplings broke. If you take the body of the train going at that rate it would destroy anything.'

When he was cross-examined on this belief Bouch floundered among his reasons until counsel remarked irritably 'Will you keep to one thing, if you please!'

Bouch's sudden, rising cry jerked the nerves of the court: '*I am explaining . . .!*'

He had not been overworried about the cracks in the columns, for he had made inquiries and found them to be a common occurrence. Some of Brunel's bridges at Chepstow were similarly cracked, and the new Severn bridge too. As for supervision of the bridge while it was building he had left that to his resident engineer Paterson, 'he had the charge of everything'.

'Would you give me an idea of how often you went there yourself.'

When changes were being made in the bridge, changes brought about by those hopelessly inaccurate river-borings 'I went there, I should say, on an average, nearly once a week, but afterwards I did not go so often. Indeed I fell ill in one year afterwards and I spent three months in the south of France.'

This had been on the advice of medical men. 'It was very much on account of anxiety in connection with this bridge.'

As he stood there in the Court answering questions he had never thought he would be asked, he fell back again and again on the unsatisfactory but honest answer 'I really cannot answer that question, for my memory does not serve me.'

But more than any involved talk of carriages and their position on the river-bed, by which Bouch sought to prove his contention that the train had dragged down his bridge, three questions damned any hope he may have had of emerging from the inquiry blameless. It is unlikely that he realized their terrible significance at the time, for they were asked at the opening of the hearing on Monday, in those first few moments before his mind became once more geared to the speed and direction of the Inquiry.

'Sir Thomas, did you in designing this bridge make any allowance at all for wind pressure?'

'Not specially.'

Here Mr Rothery's amazement was plain as he interrupted counsel. 'You made *no* allowance?'

'*Not specially.*'

'Was there not,' said Mr Trayner, 'a particular pressure had in view by you at the time you made the design?'

'I had the report of the Forth Bridge.'

But the Court knew from previous evidence that the Tay Bridge had been building for nearly three years before Bouch received this report from the Astronomer Royal, with its vague generalization about a pressure of 10 lb. to the square foot.

The incredible simplicity of Bouch's attitude to this, the key question of the Inquiry, touched the compassion of Mr Rothery, so that when the Wreck Commissioner came to ask questions about the nature of the brick and iron piers he prefaced them with words he had used to no other witness.

'I will endeavour to put them in such a way that they shall not in any way distress you, for we all have a feeling for you under the circumstances . . .'

At last the questioning was over and they let the unhappy man go. His evidence had often seemed inconsequential and prevaricating, yet he had honestly tried to assist the Court in every way he could. He had spent less time in the witness-box

than many other witnesses, and as he left the Court, joining his
wife and son and looking neither this way nor that, many
people turned their eyes away from him.

After Bouch was gone the Court sat on for another four days,
and it was not expected that the engineer would be seen again.
But, on Tuesday, 4 May, he was recalled.

The dark rumours had been current in the clubs for weeks,
and now they had reached Mr Rothery in a letter which he
could not ignore. As the Court sat on eleven o'clock he called
upon Bouch's counsel, Bidder, to make a statement.

Bidder stood up. 'You are aware, sir, that somebody has
thought fit to write to the Board of Trade drawing their attention to what he suggests is a fact material to this case; namely
that Sir Thomas Bouch is a shareholder in the firm of Hopkins,
Gilkes and Company. . .'

Bidder allowed a rustle of excitement to subside before he
continued. He said that before he called Bouch he would make
the position clear 'in half a dozen words'. It was true.. Sir
Thomas was a shareholder in that company. At this there was
an even greater murmur.

'But . . .' said Bidder, 'at the time Hopkins, Gilkes had been
contracted to build the bridge Sir Thomas had not the slightest
connection with that firm. I believe that only once in his life
had he been within the walls of their establishment.'

He had a brother, William, who had been a shareholder in the
company, and who died in January, 1876, leaving his holdings to
Sir Thomas. Bouch discovered that William, who had been a
director of the company as well, had made himself liable to the
bankers for an advance of a very large sum, something like
£13,000.

'That is the whole story,' said Mr Bidder, 'and I will just ask
Sir Thomas to step into the witness-box to confirm it.'

Gallantly Mr Trayner said that the Board of Trade had no
desire to hear confirmation from Sir Thomas. The statement
would be accepted as Mr Bidder had made it. There was no
doubt about Sir Thomas' integrity.

'At the same time,' said Mr Rothery, 'Sir Thomas *should* be called.'

So he was called, and a little of the inner faith and confidence was missing. Bewilderment showed through the cracks in the granite façade of his expression. It may have been that for the first time he had realized the temper of public feeling against him. He was questioned gently. He repeated what Bidder had already said, adding that the contractors had built many bridges for him. He said that due to the failure of the company recently he had lost 'a very large sum of money'. His brother's holdings had been £35,000, with a liability of calls for some £13,000 or more.

'But that was not the alarming thing to me, it was the obligation to the bank jointly with four other gentlemen for £100,000, and three of those other gentlemen, I think, went into liquidation or at all events were unable to meet their obligation when the work failed, and I personally along with other gentlemen became liable to the bank, and, of course, they would not let me out.'

The tragedy of the man was suddenly plain. Discredited as an engineer. His bridge in ruins. Called murderer in the gutters. Saddled with greater debts than any ordinary man could hope to pay, but unwilling to seek the ungentlemanly course of liquidation. There was complete silence as Sir Thomas Bouch left Westminster Hall, never to be seen again by the public.

The Court of Inquiry ended on 8 May 1880. It had sat for 25 non-consecutive days in Dundee and London. It had heard 120 witnesses, and it had asked 19,919 questions.

# X

*'We ought not to shrink from this duty'*

THE last sad body had long since been recovered from the Tay when the Court of Inquiry presented its report 'to both Houses of Parliament by Command of Her Majesty' in June 1880.

For reasons 'into which it is not necessary to enter' (but which the Report made quite plain) Rothery thought it better to submit his observations and his conclusions in a separate report, instead of joining with his colleagues Yolland and Barlow. When the three gentlemen sat down to consider the phrasing of their report there must have been some hard differences between them. Yolland and Barlow were both engineers, and perhaps professional sympathy, or loyalty, or caution made them reluctant to use harsh words. Not so Wreck Commissioner Henry Cadogan Rothery.

'It seems to me,' he wrote in his report, the better of the two, 'that we ought not to shrink from the duty, however painful it might be, of saying with whom the responsibility for this casualty rests ... It is our duty to say to whom it applies ... I do not understand my colleagues to differ from me in thinking that the chief blame for this casualty rests with Sir Thomas Bouch, but they consider that it is not for us to say so.'

He, however, thought it was most certainly his duty to say so, and he said so with none of the gentleness he had shown towards Bouch during the hearing.

'The conclusion then, to which we have come, is that this bridge was badly constructed and badly maintained, and that its downfall was due to inherent defects in the structure which must sooner or later have brought it down. Sir Thomas Bouch is, in our opinion, mainly to blame.'

For the faults in design ... he was entirely responsible.

For the faults in construction ... he was principally responsible.

For the faults in maintenance ... he was principally if not entirely responsible.

It had been argued that Bouch could not be judged for lack of knowledge about wind pressures when he was designing his bridge. 'Be it so,' said Rothery inexorably, 'yet he knew, or might have known, that at that time engineers in France made an allowance of 55 lb. per square foot for wind pressure, and in the United States an allowance of 50lb.'

Of the affairs at Wormit Foundry he said 'It is difficult to understand how the numerous defects should have been allowed to pass if there had been proper and competent persons to superintend the work.'

Had there been such superintendence by Bouch? 'So far as we can see, none whatever ... Sir Thomas Bouch seems to have left it to Messrs Hopkins, Gilkes & Co.; they left it to Mr Groethe, and he left it to Fergus Ferguson. With such supervision, or rather we should say with the absence of all supervision, we can hardly wonder that the columns were not cast so perfectly as they should have been, and that fatal defects in the lugs and bolt-holes should not have been pointed out.'

The best proof, Mr Rothery thought, of the total want of effective control, was afforded by the fact that one man, an unimportant man at that, had decided what thickness of metal should be used in the columns. The man, of course, was Fergus Ferguson, who had said: 'I just took it upon my own responsibility to do so. I thought it better to give an extra thickness than have them the other way.'

As for the design of the bridge it was to be regretted that Bouch had not taken greater pains to discover the nature of the river-bed on which he wanted to rest his piers. It had been argued that he was deceived by his borers. 'But what right,' wrote Rothery indignantly, 'had Sir Thomas Bouch in a matter of so much importance to trust solely to the word of the borers?'

Rothery had mercy for no one.

'We think also that Messrs Hopkins Gilkes & Co. are not free from blame for having allowed such grave irregularities to go on at Wormit foundry . . .'

'The [Railway] Company also are not free from blame for having allowed the trains to run through the High Girders at a speed greatly in excess of that which General Hutchinson had suggested as the extreme limit . . .

'Sir Thomas Bouch cannot escape his responsibility . . .'

'Sir Thomas Bouch is not relieved from his responsibility.'

Yet the report of Rothery, and the report of his colleagues did not, and admitted that they could not, explain what had happened on the night of 28 December 1879. What had brought the bridge down?

'There is no absolute knowledge of the mode in which the structure broke down,' said Yolland and Barlow.

'What probably occurred,' wrote Rothery, 'is this: the bridge had probably been strained, partly by previous gales, partly by the great speed at which trains going northward were permitted to run through the High Girders.

'The result would be that owing to the defects, to which we have called attention, the wind ties would be loosened; so that when the gale of 28th of December came on, a racking motion would be set up between the two triangular groups into which the six columns forming each pier were divided. This would bring a great additional strain upon the wind ties between the 15-inch columns which connected the two groups of columns together, and which would receive comparatively little support from the ties between the outer 18-inch and the two nearest inner columns, owing to the angle which they made with the line of pressure . . .'

And so on. But hidden behind the technicalities of the explanation was the picture of a bridge moving in a terrible gale, and moving like a troubled rope, and in that moving straining bolts and ties, testing honeycombs filled with Beaumont Egg, testing girders cast to a thickness decided by the whim of Fergus Ferguson. On to this already uneasy structure had come a train weighing almost 120 tons, shuddering under great lateral pressure from the wind.

Whether the train was, or was not, picked up and flung against the High Girders could never be known, for the evidence of witnesses, of lights falling into the river, sparks or masses of flame, was inconclusive. But in one second, which was perhaps at 7.20 p.m., the bridge could bear the agony no longer, and it broke and fell, span after span until all thirteen of the High Girders and the twelve piers that supported them had gone down into the River Tay.

For which Sir Thomas Bouch was held principally, and to some degree entirely responsible.

# FINALE

*Little man on stilts*

HE lived for four months after Mr Rothery's Report destroyed him.

His wife, Margaret, kept him to their house in Moffat and he never left it. He sat silently for the most part, and spoke to nobody of the thoughts that lay behind such silence. He received a few letters of conventional sympathy and probably answered them with courtesy. He heard nothing of the vulgar clamour for criminal proceedings against him. He was only fifty-eight years of age but his hair was white, his face the mask of an old man. His reason went so quietly from him that its passing was scarcely noticed.

He was still a member of the Institute of Civil Engineers, but the maddest of men would not now have asked him to design a kitchen wall. Trains still ran over the 300 miles of railway he had given Scotland and England. His Tay and Forth train ferries were once more in operation. Daisies and meadowsweet grew in the cuttings he had driven through the Fifeshire hills. There was much he had left behind him, and yet there was nothing because the Tay Bridge had fallen.

He had nothing to do now, and having nothing to do had no reason to go on living. So he died, with the least disturbance possible. Towards the end of October he caught a cold and had neither the strength nor the will to resist it. By half-past four on the morning of 1 November, he was dead. He was the last casualty of his rainbow bridge, the wonder bridge that had taken such ruthless payment from those who built it or used it.

Twenty men had died in its erection, and seventy-five men and women and children in its fall.

The first contractor had died before his contract could be

taken up. The second went insane and also died. The third was ruined by the disaster.

Bouch's resident engineer, William Paterson, whose son had so blithely laid the foundation stone, was struck down by a paralysis from which he never recovered, the result of his 'attention and anxiety about the bridge'.

And then, finally, Sir Thomas Bouch, first gently mad and then dead, too.

Death is often regarded as a tragedy, which it is not in itself, no matter how violent or unexpected it may be, or how many people it may choose to take at one moment. Tragedy is not a word that has been used in this book to describe the deaths of sweet Jessie Bain, or wee Davie Macdonald of the penny pencil, or to describe the picture of a blind brother gently touching the dead face of Robert Watson.

But it is used now for Thomas Bouch. It is a tragedy when a man destroys himself, not willingly, not as an act of suicide, but in reaching beyond his abilities. Thomas Bouch was a little man on stilts. His century, his country, arrogant and upward-reaching, was full of such men, and life tolerantly permitted most of them to totter through to natural death. But the Great Storm of 28 December blew the stilts from beneath Thomas Bouch, as cynically as it plucked the stilts from beneath his bridge.

As for Henry Abel Noble, 'no better examiner of concrete and Portland cement' could probably have been found. This would have been enough of a distinction to satisfy most ordinary men, and might have satisfied Noble had not greater responsibility been thrust upon him. His tragedy, if it was a tragedy, lay in his failure to realize the absurdity of leaving a great bridge in his charge.

A rusty death on the beach at Tayport was not the end of engine 224. She was sent to Cowlairs, where she was repaired and refitted and set once more upon rails. And on the rails she continued to work for another forty-five years. Her drivers were proud of her. They called her 'The Diver'.

One by one in the years that followed the disaster the High

Girders were lifted from the bed of the river. Dynamite was used to blast many of them from the grasp of the gravel. They were sold as scrap to an English company of locomotive engineers which made them into railway engines. Each engine carried a small plate recording the origin of its metal. Until a year or so ago one of these tiny, serviceable engines was still in use in southern Spain.

The Relief Fund continued to operate. One of the last dependants to apply for aid was a man called Mitchell, David Mitchell, who asked for assistance in 1938. In 1879 he had been eight years of age, and his father had been the driver of the 5.20 from Burntisland.

The last application of all was made just before the war by Miss Janet Patterson Scott. She was in receipt of the Old Age Pension, she said, and she also received £16 a year in interest on her savings, but since this was all she had to live upon she would appreciate help from the Fund.

She was seventy-four years in age, and to support her claim she produced two brass buttons, neatly tied together with black ribbon. Her brother had been George Scott, one of the two guards who travelled to duty on the 5.20. Two days before the disaster and his death he had cut the buttons from his uniform and given them to his sister.

Before the directors of the Fund could make a decision Miss Scott died gently at St Andrews.

*Minster Lovell*
*December 1955*

# ACKNOWLEDGEMENTS

To write a book like this would be impossible without help. It took two years to gather all the material that made it, and much patience from the many people who answered my questions, threw open their records, or diligently searched for facts that I later may have discarded as irrelevant. To name them all would not be practicable, but I particularly wish to record my gratitude to the following:

Thomas Bouch, of Ashorne, grandson of the designer.
The Reverend C. M. L. Bouch, of Cumberland.
L. C. Johnston, Archivist to the British Transport Comm.
John Cameron, of the *Dundee Courier & Advertiser.*
Ian Stewart, of the *Dundee Courier & Advertiser.*
A. E. Jennings, of Valentine & Sons, Ltd.
The Superintendent of Police, Dundee.
The Town Clerk, Dundee.
The Chief Librarian, Dundee.
H. A. Vallance, of *The Railway Magazine.*
H. M. Hunter, British Railways, Scottish Region.
Ronald Russell.
C. Hamilton Ellis.
The Royal Geographical Society, and the Institute of Civil Engineers.

The doggerel used for some chapter headings is taken from contemporary ballads. All quotations, except where otherwise plain, are from the Dundee and national Press, and from evidence given before the Court of Inquiry.

John Prebble

## MORE ABOUT PENGUINS
## AND PELICANS

*Penguinews*, which appears every month, contains details of all the new books issued by Penguins as they are published. It is supplemented by our stocklist which includes around 5,000 titles.

A specimen copy of *Penguinews* will be sent to you free on request. Please write to Dept EP, Penguin Books Ltd, Harmondsworth, Middlesex, for your copy.

*In the U.S.A.*: For a complete list of books available from Penguins in the United States write to Dept CS, Penguin Books, 625 Madison Avenue, New York, New York 10022.

*In Canada*: For a complete list of books available from Penguins in Canada write to Penguin Books Canada Ltd, 2801 John Street, Markham, Ontario L3R 1B4.